American Impressions

ALSO BY RIVA CASTLEMAN

Contemporary Prints
Technics and Creativity: Gemini G. E. L.
Prints of the Twentieth Century: A History
Printed Art: A View of Two Decades
Prints from Blocks: Gauguin to Now

American Impressions
PRINTS SINCE POLLOCK

Riva Castleman

Alfred A. Knopf ✦ New York · 1985

THIS IS A BORZOI BOOK

PUBLISHED BY ALFRED A. KNOPF, INC.

Library of Congress Cataloging in Publication Data
Castleman, Riva.   American impressions.
Bibliography: p.
Includes index.
1. Prints, American—Themes, motives. 2. Prints—20th century—
United States—Themes, motives. I. Title.
NE508.C365   1985   769.973   84-47690
ISBN 0-394-53683-5

Manufactured in Japan

FIRST EDITION

LIST OF ILLUSTRATIONS

ACKNOWLEDGMENTS

Just before this book was begun, a remarkable era in American art came to an end. Tatyana Grosman, who encouraged and inspired artists to make prints at the most auspicious historical moment, slowly and finally succumbed to a series of illnesses. With words she penned to my distinguished predecessor at the Museum of Modern Art, William S. Lieberman, I would like to acknowledge the valuable assistance I received from the generous people listed below, and from those many experts, colleagues, and artists who shared their insights and opinions with me over the years. She wrote: "I am so very thankful to you for your understanding, for all the kind and wise help you have given me with much heart."

Matthew Marks

Porter McCray

Dorothy C. Miller

June Wayne

Clinton Adams (University of New Mexico)

Janet Flint (National Museum of American Art)

Judith Goldman (Whitney Museum of American Art)

Sanford Hirsch (Adolph and Esther Gottlieb Foundation)

David W. Kiehl (Metropolitan Museum of Art)

Joann Moser (University of Iowa Museum of Art)

Robert Rainwater (New York Public Library)

Andrew Stasik (Pratt Graphic Art Center)

Richard Tooke (Museum of Modern Art)

Brooke Alexander

Sylvan Cole, Jr.

Rosa Esman

William Goldston (Universal Limited Art Editions, Inc.)

Marion Goodman (Multiples, Inc.)

Ken Tyler

Douglas Baxter (Paula Cooper Gallery)

Theodore A. Bonin (Brooke Alexander, Inc.)

Cee Scott Brown (Holly Solomon Editions, Ltd.)

Diane Buci (Parasol Press)

Lisa E. David (Fendrick Gallery)

Carl Hecker (David Anderson Gallery)

Hiroshi (Simca Press)

Shirley Irons (Barbara Gladstone Gallery)

Ann and Jack Lemmon (Landfall Press)

Karen McCready (Crown Point Press)

Jean Milant (Cirrus Editions)

Robert Monk (Castelli Graphics)

Carl Solway

Tami Swett (Petersburg Press, Inc.)

Ann Tullis (Experimental Workshop)

Joni Weyl (Gemini G.E.L.)

Giovanna Zamboni (Contemporary
Graphic Centre Services, Inc.)

Whatever clarity and grace this book has is due to the knowledgeable skills of its editor, Susan Ralston, who fortunately is an avid collector of contemporary American prints as well. Her enthusiasm for the subject sharpened and amplified my impressions of how printmaking developed in the United States. Should it happen that these impressions occasionally mistake reality, remembered or even documented, the art itself can be depended upon to reveal the most exact truth.

American Impressions

INTRODUCTION

". . . just as in politics, revolutionary ideas in art, after they are generally accepted, become a part of conservative opinion which in turn has to defend itself against a new revolution."

—ALFRED H. BARR, JR.[1]

The rapidity of change that has impressed itself upon even the least conscious member of society has colored all facts and surmises about what has occurred since World War II. Machines have had to augment the limited storage capacity of human brains in order to keep track of the glut of information that requires retention and retrieval. And yet, for all the filed and digested data, the objective view of even the recent past is still murky, disjointed, and twisted. Time, which nicely compresses our memories of events and things, composes history for us. The vibrant ideas of artists often rise up from this convenient sandwiching of the past, sometimes abrasive in their capacity to reveal truths about the life of their time and of our present. Tracing those ideas is difficult, for there is no one line that links them, and their meanings are often prophetic and obscure.

In an age of overabundant visual imagery, dealing with one form of art, prints, that has contributed to the massive backlog, is a gargantuan undertaking. Prints, after all, have long been a means of disseminating artistic ideas, and it was probably inevitable that their quantity should increase in proportion to other visual forms. It is, therefore, of some use to examine a portion of the prints issued during four decades of informational overload in order to obtain some sense of how artists responded to this era. Understandably, the selection of prints to be discussed has been made from a viewpoint already distorted by faded personal memories of the period. No historian lives in a vacuum, and an objective study of even unfamiliar objects is impossible.

Assessments of the recent past depend upon blind courage and acute sensitivity to the texture of accumulated material. Other ages have been just as overwhelmed by increase, whether in ideas, goods, or populations; decrease is rarely the subject of discourse. But is the period following World War II significantly different? Notably, culture has been embraced by people who may, in another age, have never looked at a picture as a work of art. The camera, radio, and motion picture have brought about acquaintance with a broad range of objects and ideas in only a century. In his illuminating survey *Future Shock,* Alvin Toffler writes, "Important new machines do more than suggest or compel changes in other machines. . . . They alter man's total intellectual environment—the way he thinks and looks at the world."[2] Television gave private access to a considerably greater variety of experience, and into this nearly universal situation the artist had to contribute worthy ideas. The large number of prints that American artists produced, particularly during the 1960s and '70s, played a vital role in offering these ideas to a larger mass of receptive viewers than had existed anywhere, ever.

When generous statements about artistic print production are made, the commercial interests that have affected most of its aspects must be taken into consideration. There is no question that American society from 1944 onward became blatantly consumerized, and notwithstanding the frustration of youth—manifested in civil disruptions during the same period—it was inevitable that works of artists had to play a part in all levels of that society. In retrospect, it is clear that the dialectic which Alfred H. Barr, Jr., offered as an absolute truth has been prolonged in its inexorable revolutionary path as pluralism in taste has diffused the concept of avant-gardism.

Before discussion of the period beginning around 1960, when prints began to form a major presence in the world of art, the stage for the dramatic change in the attitude of painters and sculptors toward the print mediums must be set. In part, history reflects the American artist's reconciliation with both machines and society, and perhaps the real revolution has taken place in the way artists work. However, this particular history will recount only a small portion of the so-called print revolution, emphasizing the ways painters and sculptors have encountered and often conquered the print mediums. Because it is their work alone that may be preserved and praised in the future, the means by which it has been accomplished, contributing subtly to its shape and content and usually lost in the compression of time, have deliberately been given an imbalance of emphasis. This then is the story of how American artists came to make prints that covered the globe. It is a tale not quite as real as the art itself.

CHAPTER ONE

When Jackson Pollock entered the New York shop of S. W. Hayter in 1944 he must have had some inkling that he had finally made contact with history. Thoroughly American, as only a Westerner could be, Pollock had been well programmed in the 1930s with middle-American values and acceptable aesthetic policies by the most dedicated of the regionalist artists, Thomas Hart Benton, with whom he studied at New York's Art Students League. Another side of the New York art environment was characterized by emigré artists like Arshile Gorky, the Mexican muralists, and the blue-ribbon European art promulgated by the Museum of Modern Art. After some exposure to these influences, Pollock was beginning to work toward imagery that spun out from social realism into an extremely personal representation of objects and people that had its basis in Surrealism and in Picasso's work of the 1930s. It was at this moment that he decided to try his hand at engraving at Atelier 17, the print workshop that Hayter had transferred from Paris, where students and experienced artists worked side by side.

Hayter had developed a method of expressing some of the Surrealist spirit through the means of automatic drawing. When making an engraving, Hayter would randomly move the plate around as he pushed his engraving tool (burin). From the masses of curved lines that resulted he would pick out figurative elements, reinforcing them with further engraving and etching (Fig. 1). His subjects in the 1930s had close parallels with those of Picasso and Masson, so it is little wonder that his own enthusiasm for the Surrealist spirit was conveyed to most of those who visited Atelier 17. Like many others, Hayter had been forced to flee the Nazis. The printshop he set up in New York became a central meeting place for many of the European artists who had also escaped; quite a few actually worked at Atelier 17 before returning to Europe after the war. Plates by Chagall, Masson, and Tanguy that were destined for the *VVV* portfolio (1943) were made at Hayter's shop.

In this milieu, Jackson Pollock briefly sought to translate the Hayter method of image-making into a group of prints based on his own personal subjects (Figs. 2, 3). Most of the prints were not much more than sketches that had been subjected to a second or third touch-up. Because it is difficult to see what has been scratched into a plate until a printed proof is taken, most of the first markings only begin to describe what the artist is getting at. Certainly, with Hayter's method, there could be no conscious effort to create a finished composition in the first state. Pollock tried to extend the subconscious markings into further states, rarely doing as Hayter had done—picking out figures and forms and tearing them away from the masses of flowing but meaningless lines. In a few plates figures have been drawn, immediately indicating the direction of the composition. Pollock was not keen on clarifying the figures at the expense of the indeterminate lines. He allowed the all-over pattern of swirling lines to have an importance equal to the few areas that he chose to detail.

In 1942 Pollock had met the brilliant, well-educated Robert Motherwell, who tried to get him to exhibit with some of the Surrealists whose friendship Motherwell had been cultivating since his arrival in New York in 1940. (Pollock did not participate in the exhibition, although he had been included in a showing of French and American artists earlier that year, when one reviewer wrote, "Pollock resembles Hayter . . ."[3]) Along with several other artists who were then working at Atelier 17 on prints for the *VVV* portfolio, Motherwell was attempting to produce his first etchings. Evidently his printmaking efforts were discouraging, for his eventual contribution to the portfolio was a series of watercolors.

In the spring of 1943, Pollock and Motherwell made collages together and exhibited them at Peggy Guggenheim's gallery, Art of This Century. Although Pollock met Hayter in Provincetown that summer, it was probably Motherwell who was instrumental in bringing Pollock to work at Atelier 17. Hayter has said that Pollock met the Surrealist André Masson at the workshop, but that they probably did not discuss art, since neither artist spoke the other's language. On the other hand, Motherwell, having spent some time in France and being eager to learn everything about Surrealism, was an important conduit of Surrealist philosophy and gossip. Much of his aesthetic formation was being molded by his friendships. He consciously tried to introduce Surrealist methods into his and Pollock's work, although Pollock had already discovered a kind of automatism through psychoanalysis and had assimilated it rather less self-consciously into his progressively more abstract style.

By the fall of 1944, Pollock had had his first one-man show at Peggy Guggenheim's, had sold his first painting to the Museum of Modern Art, was on a monthly stipend from his new dealer, and had begun his work at Atelier 17. He continued spasmodically to work there into 1945. During this period the workshop was moved from the New School for Social Research to a building on Eighth Street and a larger press was installed. It was on this larger press that Pollock made his most evolved compositions in engraving.

The several plates that Pollock had engraved in 1944–45 were packed away when he moved to a small farmhouse in Springs, Long Island, with his new wife, Lee Krasner, in November 1945. No editions had been taken of the prints, nor, probably, were they ever referred to by the artist. While Pollock later approved some serigraphs made after his black and white paintings, he never again tried his hand at printmaking. Like many other American artists, he had made lithographs in the 1930s, so it was not lack of technique that kept him away from the printing press. It is evident, however, that living far from any workshop, disdaining group activity (his excuse for not participating in the Surrealist exhibition of 1942), and a deepening of his commitment to the active method of Abstract Expressionist painting, which was so absolutely individual in attitude, removed most possibilities of making prints. Ironically, his death in August 1956 was nearly coincidental with the opening of a print workshop on Long Island, Universal Limited Art Editions (ULAE), the leading vehicle of the print explosion of the 1960s.

Pollock's experience with printmaking was little different from that of other painters who were to become known as America's first internationally renowned school, Abstract Expressionism. The few examples of printmaking among this group, as each artist was developing a mature style, were made either at Atelier 17 (William Baziotes, Robert Motherwell, Mark Rothko) or on the individual's own small etching press (Adolph Gottlieb). Motherwell learned more about etching in the studio of the émigré Surrealist artist Kurt Seligmann (Fig. 5), but never really pursued the medium until the late 1960s. A few of the new abstract artists eventually did participate in the creation of a portfolio that developed under the aegis of Atelier 17, after Hayter's return to Paris in 1950. Still, the prints of Franz Kline and Willem de Kooning that appeared in this ambitious album, *21 Etchings and Poems,* were souvenirs rather than commitments to the medium of etching. This lack of attraction to the print mediums in America by the foremost artists of the post-war period has to be put into context.

There are several aspects of art production in America in the 1940s and '50s that clarify the dearth of printed art by this group, and most of them are firmly attached to the transformed social and economic conditions in America after World War II. Most of the artists who were to have their greatest development and renown during this period had been employed by the Federal Art Project (FAP) during the 1930s. This allowed them to continue working at a time when any full-time job outside the field of art (should it have been available) would have exhausted all the creative energies they might have had. The Depression was, in and of itself, a time of total exhaustion—the drain of energy exacerbated by fear of even worse days to come. When the United States entered the war in 1941, the artists who were later to have the most importance were all in their thirties or late twenties, the age-group first to be drafted. As it happened, only one of these developing artists was actively involved in the war: Ad Reinhardt, who pursued the semiprofessional job of photographer for the Navy. Pollock and Motherwell, the other leading "young" artists, were both classified 4-F. They stayed home, interacting with the established European artists who took refuge in America, participating in exhibitions, and using other aspects of this unique situation to their advantage.

The center of experiment in the 1940s was Atelier 17 (partly because of the working presence there of European artists, but also because engraving and other intaglio techniques such as etching, drypoint, and aquatint had simply not been exploited by serious American artists since the 1920s). A meeting place for the displaced professional European painters and a school for young printmakers, Hayter's workshop also attracted men like Gabor Peterdi (Fig. 8), who had worked in the Paris Atelier 17, and Mauricio Lasansky (Fig. 7), who had developed his own intaglio technique in Argentina and continued his work in the New York shop. Peterdi and Lasansky signaled a change in the perception of printmaking and the manner in which artists would be educated in post-war America.

Peterdi was a painter and a printmaker who had, gypsy-like, wandered from his native Hungary across Europe to Paris, participating in the activities of the Surrealists for a short while before the Occupation. He used Hayter's techniques with great skill and turned them into a complex personal style. After the 1940s he continued his work at Yale University, where two generations of art students carried on the printmaking philosophy that was initially brought to America by Hayter.

Lasansky went to the State University of Iowa in 1945, to set up an intaglio workshop with a teaching program based somewhat on that of Atelier 17. In order to direct his students away from an academic delineation of form, Lasansky purged the workshop of its remnants of American provincialism: the lithographic stones and presses that were the means of carrying on the spirit of its famous local representative, Grant Wood, were relegated to dead storage.

"Printmaker!" The connotation of this word, curiously absent from other languages, began to have some meaning only after World War II. Surely, before the war, and often in the long, splendid history of prints, there had been artists who created nothing but prints. However, in most cases the artists drew a composition before going to the plate or block or stone, rather than working directly on these materials exclusively. Even this is not the entire distinction between earlier artists like Callot and Meryon and those followers of Hayter who could only be called "printmakers." Callot and Meryon made prints that, following the original object of working in a multiple medium, were meant to be printed in large numbers for wide distribution of the image. Indeed, many painters made prints for this sole reason. But the printmakers of the second half of the twentieth century have found that creating in a print medium is itself totally satisfying; they often care not at all if no more than a few copies are made before they go on to the next image. It is the complex techniques of printmaking that entrance them. In the words of Sylvan Cole, former Director of Associated American Artists (AAA, the largest print gallery in America and publisher of over 1,500 prints since 1934), "The change that . . . was taking place was the breakup with the artist/painter (or Abstract Expressionist) who was not interested in printmaking, and out of this came a man called a printmaker . . . people like Karl Schrag, Peterdi, Lasansky, Misch Kohn—who built their reputations as printmakers."[4]

Before the war, in the workshops of the FAP, artists made considerable numbers of prints. This was their only work; no doubt it was often a matter of survival, not preference. Dozens of prints in a relatively new medium, silkscreen, were turned out for the adornment of schools and other government buildings. While artists who regularly worked in the printshops of the FAP created few memorable images, they did collect wages and they did set the foundation for later, more profound commitments to the print mediums.

The G.I. Bill filled the colleges, universities, and art schools of post-war America during a period of prosperity that encouraged such institutions to enlarge their facilities or open new ones, particularly those devoted to the arts. Many veterans who would never have had the opportunity of attending college if they had not been drafted had little direction—were "lost," so to speak—and found that the unrestrained atmosphere of the post-war art schools and art departments represented just the sort of freedom they needed after years of military conformity. (Many others, of course, had profited from the organized lifestyle of the military and sought it in more disciplined fields such as law, medicine, and business. The famous "Organization Man" could hardly have had such success if this less independent group had not also made a major contribution to post-war society.) In the late 1940s, then, one could observe the beginnings of a phenomenal expansion of art education in institutions of higher learning, where art departments attracted returning G.I.s who had completed their undergraduate work before the war, and in older, established art schools that were filled to capacity with those who had only finished high school. Students who fell under the spell of Lasansky during his first years at the State University of Iowa went on to found print workshops in other universities. Soon students of these workshops pioneered others, so that in a very short time there were facilities for the study of printmaking (and this usually meant intaglio) in most universities in the United States.

The proliferation of places where printmaking was taught and the subsequent increase in the number of printmakers led to the birth of ancillary institutions: the Brooklyn Museum's annual National Print Exhibition (begun in 1947), an open exhibition, in contrast with the traditional invitational showings of the Society of Etchers (note that these artists referred to themselves as etchers, not printmakers) or the other one-medium groups such as the National Serigraph Society; the International Group Arts Society, a membership/subscription organization the purpose of which was to publish and sell prints by new artists of less conservative nature than those sponsored by AAA; and regional and international exhibitions devoted exclusively to prints, such as the Northwest Printmakers Society, the Philadelphia Print Club, and international biennials of prints in Cincinnati (1950), Ljubljana (1955), and Tokyo (1957). Thus, in the United States and elsewhere, the need to show and distribute the outpourings of the print workshops produced new organizations that in turn further encouraged the creation of prints.

The American artist not only survived but prevailed in the late 1940s, rubbing shoulders with the Surrealists in New York, finding some points of communication with them but retaining enough national ego and spirit to endure the continual barrage of European superiority. Parisian-made art ceased to be the ideal, and critics, institutions, and ultimately the public recognized that another world war had been won, at last. It was now possible for American artists to look far more widely for motifs, subjects, points of view. Underlying most of this acceptance of possible foreign influences was a multifaceted competition to find imagery equal to the powerful personality of European art and to assimilate some of its philosophical foundation. To Breton's dictatorial Surrealist pronouncements were added the more engaging existential arguments of Jean-Paul Sartre. In this climate the dreamlike inspiration of Surrealism was only one influence on the emerging artist; the shock of heightened reality perceived in the relatively little-known works of the German Expressionists was given close examination as well.

Most of the Surrealists were French, and all of them lived in France until the

Nazi troops took control in 1940. However, German refugees had been arriving in America since 1932. A few had found new homes in other European countries before it was necessary to flee the continent altogether, and some, like Max Beckmann (who had first gone to Holland), decided that it might be better to spend some time in America after the war than to return immediately to Germany. Most of the Bauhaus masters—Josef Albers, Lyonel Feininger, Walter Gropius, and Ludwig Mies van der Rohe—had arrived in America in the 1930s after the dissolution of the school, and attempted to continue some part of their pioneering work in the United States. Albers, who played a pivotal role as an instructor at Black Mountain College from 1933 to 1949, made a group of offset lithographs while he was a visiting professor at Harvard in 1942. The prints of his *Graphic Tectonic* (Fig. 15) are mechanical drawings, made with the tools of a designer. They are measured, structured works, descended from the type of geometrical abstraction that developed in part during the Russian Revolution, as a means of making signs that were comprehensible to all. Indeed, Albers was convinced that man-made was better than machine-made, and that art was meant to be serviceable. The series of compositions made up of concentric sets of linear enclosures was itself of little importance in the mainstream of art thought during the 1940s, but the concept behind them was indicative of yet another influential presence of European culture in America.

What was probably most important to the post-war awakening of interest in German art in America was the advent here of Max Beckmann in 1947. His work had been shown regularly at the Bucholz Gallery in New York during the war years, and in 1946 its director, Curt Valentin, had published Beckmann's final prints, a set of transfer lithographs titled *Day and Dream* (Fig. 9), on the occasion of his exhibition of Beckmann's wartime paintings. In 1948 his first American retrospective was shown in St. Louis and subsequently traveled to Los Angeles, Detroit, Baltimore, and Minneapolis. Eventually, after two years in St. Louis, Beckmann moved to New York, where he lived the last year and a half before his death. He was considered the greatest living German artist, a reputation underscored by his representation in New York by Valentin, who was also Picasso's American dealer. It is no wonder that young artists seeking more subjective imagery would be drawn to Beckmann and to other Germans who only became known in America around 1950, when American Occupation troops began returning from Europe.

The affinity with the medium of woodcut exhibited by many artists of the 1950s derived from several sources other than the example of the German Expressionists. Lithography, the main print medium of the 1930s, still had its practitioners in the old established workshops of New York and Los Angeles, but it demanded a good deal of expertise in preparing the stones and printing, and physically was almost impossible to produce without assistance—and assistance was almost impossible to procure without cash, always in short supply. (The students in Hayter's shop, including Pollock, had to pull their own prints, which explains very well why there were no editions of Pollock's engravings during his lifetime.) Woodcut, on the other hand, was an intensely personal medium. The woodblock never had to leave the artist's studio, from the moment of the first cut to the completion of the final prints. Not even a press was needed, since the prints could be taken simply by rubbing the back of a piece of paper pressed against the inked surface of the block. This was exactly the type of work American artists favored: a mixture of personal expression, handicraft, and cost efficiency.

In 1950, when the Brooklyn Museum mounted "American Woodcut: 1670–1950," it included the work of some contemporary artists with some expertise in the medium, such as Antonio Frasconi (from Uruguay, who had begun to make woodcuts there in 1944), Adja Yunkers (who arrived from Stockholm after the war [Fig. 18]), and Josef Albers. Central to the teaching of woodcut in the New York area was Louis Schanker (Fig. 17), an American abstract painter who, with Adolph Gottlieb and Mark Rothko, was a member of "The Ten" in the late 1930s. In the 1940s he taught printmaking at the New School for Social Research and for one year shared his workshop with Hayter. Although Schanker taught woodcut, he did make some etchings with Hayter during this period. It is known, however, that Hayter had a strong aversion to woodcut (he refused to continue being a member of the Society of American Etchers if they admitted any "woodpeckers").[5] It is not known if Adolph Gottlieb's few woodcuts of 1944–45 were the result of his earlier association with Schanker, but it is certain that Schanker was probably the most direct tie to the burgeoning interest in woodcut in the 1950s. His workshop was home to young artists, such as the sculptor Leonard Baskin, who must have considered the precious Surrealist methods implicit in the Hayter method out of step with the times.

Before further examination of the development of American printmaking, mention should be made of the Europeans, who dominated the American art scene and created a few prints in the United States. At Atelier 17, prints were occasionally made by André Masson, Yves Tanguy (Fig. 10) and Jacques Lipchitz (Fig. 11)—both of whom remained in America—Max Ernst, Marc Chagall, Joan Miró and Salvador Dali (both of whom worked in the shop after the war), and Matta (who, rather younger than the better established artists, was friendly with the Americans).

That peripatetic sculptor Alexander Calder, who divided his life between France and America until 1938 and after 1948, made most of his early etchings with Hayter. With many of the European artists he contributed to the *VVV* portfolio, creating a prophetic engraving at Atelier 17 (Fig. 12). Calder's print, probably confusing and illegible even to knowledgeable viewers, was a notation for the movement of a mobile sculpture. This schematic work, with precedent in typographical publications of the Constructivists and Bauhaus artists, must certainly have seemed, to some, an unthinkable theme for an American art object. On the other hand, Calder, with his less-than-serious wire circus performances, was a unique artist. He had longtime friendships and acquaintances among the Europeans, but not exclusively among the Surrealists, and exhibited at the Bucholz Gallery during the war years, alongside painters as different as Beckmann and Masson.

Calder lived in Connecticut, near the homes of Julien Levy, who ran a gallery in New York specializing in Surrealist art during the 1930s and '40s, and Arshile Gorky. Other displaced artists such as Masson, Tanguy, and Naum Gabo also sought the peace and quiet of Connecticut. Gabo had come from England after the war, quietly producing a long and inventive series of wood engravings, executed as monoprints, from 1950 to 1973 (Fig. 14). While both Calder's and Gabo's unusual printmaking projects fell into the limbo reserved for peripheral creations of major artists, they may now be seen as significant precursors of two art forms adopted with considerable zeal in the 1970s: Conceptual Art and monotype.

In 1952, in connection with an exhibition at the Philadelphia Museum of Art titled "A Decade of American Printmaking," Kneeland McNulty, the assistant curator of prints, wrote in the *Museum Bulletin*:

> There is no doubt that the discovery of new techniques and experimentation with old are stimulating experiences in themselves, and ones which can and do produce great art. However, the danger inherent in experimentation for its own self is implicit in some of the print work of today. . . . Technique, for the sake of technique, is apt to destroy the essence of art itself. It cannot be the end to which it is also the means. This was a period of transition, reflecting a change from say, the art of Arms, Heintzelman and Gropper, to that of Hayter, Pollock and Shahn.[6]

McNulty's distrust of experimentation in technique was based on his fear that artists were on the way to reproducing their paintings—or creating surrogates for paintings—in their prints. His inclusion of Ben Shahn among the newer printmakers is of particular interest because Shahn's serigraphs (all silkscreen prints by artists were formally referred to as serigraphs by McNulty's boss, Curator Carl Zigrosser) carefully reproduced, for the most part, the subjects of his paintings of the 1930s. Although Shahn's painting style later changed radically from social-protest realism to a style reflecting Surrealist inspiration, he never made prints exactly in this later manner.

What McNulty was referring to when he mentioned Shahn was the burgeoning of color prints that had occurred since 1942. It is difficult to realize how few prints were executed in color in America before the experiments conducted in the FAP workshops in the late 1930s, particularly by the artists working in silkscreen. There had been a few color woodcuts made after 1918 and into the 1920s by Max Weber, but these were not generally known. "Pop" Hart had experimented with monotype etchings in color and made at least one color lithograph in 1929. Less ambitious works in color woodcut were common among amateur artists, but painters, in general, had taken the traditional black and white to be the most suitable form for prints prior to their FAP experiences. A number of color lithographs were included in the Philadelphia exhibition, again prompting McNulty to fret about the competition with painting. Size, too, had been increasing; all the more reason to worry about the preservation of the print as a distinct art form.

The impact of refugee artists in America, particularly in the New York area but also around Los Angeles where many writers and musicians had settled, was greatest during World War II and to the end of the 1940s. American artists had been prepared for it, no matter that little discourse could occur directly between them and the newcomers. The experience of the work programs during the Depression had kept them "tuned up," ready to take advantage of extreme situations. "The subservience . . . to chauvinistic and ideological aims"[7] represented by regionalism and social realism was a local situation in which they already struggled. But for some artists, confrontation with those great personalities that dominated art, even in America, was as much a battle as that going on in Europe. In the words of Ad Reinhardt, "The one struggle in art is the struggle of artists against artists."[8] The most talented American artists were literally forced to find a form that could overwhelm the opposition, but in that struggle the main energies went into painting and sculpture, not into prints.

A few lessons were learned through prints, but an expanded art audience was not yet ready for the new forms, and the artists could not spare the time to wage that battle, too. What prints did emerge came from painters and sculptors already grounded in technique and mature in style. Younger Americans who created woodcuts and intaglio prints at this time were interested in the print mediums to such an extent that they did all their exploration there. Unlike the painters, they did not feel embattled, and the potency of their images will probably never be as significant. The few exceptional printed images of the period, even continuing into the 1950s, were made by artists such as Albers and Gabo, foreigners whose battles were already fought and won.

In the post-war era, the competition for supremacy in art was waged by thirty- and forty-year-old artists against a foreign adversary. The next generation's provocateur would be not only the Abstract Expressionist's image but all images. The nemesis of all visual expression was the novel machine that changed nearly every possible attitude about the communication of ideas, their form and content: television.

CHAPTER TWO

The second decade after the war was a time for serious assessment of the new world order and of the human environment. The 1950s and early 1960s were rife with lengthy discussions of how things had changed. For the most part, scholars were concerned with understanding the particulars of existence under the deluge of information to which they so abundantly contributed. Because he captured the popular ear and eye, Marshall McLuhan, more than any other expert on the subject, was able to provide a method of comprehending the prevalent informational overload. Television was a phenomenon which was only partially understood, but McLuhan, in promoting his own view of its impact upon American society,[9] programmed a larger public than was ever previously possible to think about its implications. While it was amusing to repeat his slogan, "The medium is the message," and apply it to other aspects of the mechanization of human activity, it was increasingly clear that television had become the critical component in daily life.

Conscious visual choice, until the advent of television, had been considered a matter of deciding what to look at and when. It rarely occurred to anyone that whenever one's eyes were open visual choices were being made with such rapidity that it would be impossible to rethink an event and put into sequence each selection. The conscious visual choice as regards television is to have one to look at, or not to have one at all; the selection of what is to be looked at is, in this sense, irrelevant. Whatever is seen will be simply an addition to the mass of messages received during any period when the eyes are open. It matters little what may appear when the television is on: a pattern or station-identifying logo, the flopping of an image, or the ordinary transmission of a soap opera, game show, movie, or newscast.

During the early years of visual overload, the mature Abstract Expressionists of the New York School were making their most important works. They had grown up during a less complex period; now their confrontation was not with the machinery but with the psyche that had to endure it. The imagination needed exercise, and for those who were willing to look, abstract painting provided the means. Much younger artists who were just beginning their careers in the 1950s were also required to face up to the changed nature of looking and to produce works that exploited simultaneity and other aspects of perception that had been brought closer to the conscious surface. Between the two groups was a third that was as pluralistic as the American melting pot.

Taking as an example the first comprehensive survey of twentieth-century American work that was seen in Europe after the war, "Modern Art in the United States," organized by the Museum of Modern Art in 1955, it is possible to see the diversity of post-war artistic expression and observe the position of prints in that context. Of the approximately twenty-five pre-war artists represented, more than half had made prints; only five of the nearly thirty-two contemporary painters had made prints (usually one or two), but none of these was included in the exhibition. The section devoted to contemporary prints presented forty-eight artists, mainly printmakers, one-third of whom had been influenced or taught by S. W. Hayter. Slightly more than a third of the works exhibited were color woodcuts, five were lithographs (three in color), and three were silkscreens; all were made between 1945 and 1954, with the meaningful exception of one of Josef Albers's offset lithographs from the 1942 series *Graphic Tectonic* (Fig. 15).

It is useful to examine this exhibition in order to find some reasons for the near-eclipse of the type of printmaking represented in it that occurred around 1960, when painters began to include lithography and silkscreen as principal elements in their total creative activity. These prints display most of the modernist stylistic trends of the 1920s and '30s. The figurative works are pointedly neither social realist nor provincial (the two modes no longer acceptable as fine or modern art). Most of the prints have Surrealist or Expressionist foundations, with derivations from Ernst, Masson, and Picasso permeating a good deal of the imagery. Because most were created by printmakers who had not fully digested the influences from abroad, there are few substantive images, although the prints are well executed. The predominating impressions are those of tactility and color. In the intaglio prints of Peterdi, Lasansky, and their students, and in the woodcuts of Frasconi, Schanker, and Yunkers, there is an insistent emphasis upon texture, as the deeply engraved or etched lines and harshly grained wood prevail over the weaker imagery. Technique is a primary concern and the excitement of working with new or unusual materials—such as embedding wires into wood, or cutting into plastic—overwhelms most of the profound aesthetic elements.

The new generation looked at existing prints as sources of new ideas for their own creations. For example, in 1949 Rolf Nesch, a German artist directly influenced by E. L. Kirchner and who worked in Norway during and after World War II, had a show in New York of his intricate multi-panel works, printed from assemblages of wire, metal scrap, Masonite, and other such materials, prompting many other artists to attempt to mix mediums in similar ways. Often the plates became low-relief sculptures, and the resulting embossed prints seemed imprisoned when shown behind glass. Still, more and more printmakers tried to find ways of making deeper and deeper reliefs of their prints, seeking some manner of execution that would be tantalizingly new.

Color, of course, was the most seductive of the trends in printmaking. The silkscreen and color lithograph experiments of the FAP were known primarily among the artists who made them and the schoolchildren and hospital patients who, coming across them in the halls or rooms of their public facilities, occasionally looked at them. Most of these prints were meant to be no more than wall decorations with pleasant or social messages; color was used to attract the eyes of viewers who were less sophisticated than those who normally looked at contemporary pictures. The serious development of color prints coincided with the growing interest in woodcutting, which allowed for experimentation in ways that other mediums did not. The examples of the German Expressionists, Edvard Munch, and Paul Gauguin became better known, and printmakers began more and more to ink their blocks with color.

The freshest new influence seems to have come from Japan, but not necessarily only from the famous Ukiyo-e prints. The Japanese people were seen in their own country for the first time by considerable numbers of impressionable young Americans—soldiers on duty in Japan with the Army of the Occupation—and their daily lives and surroundings were discovered to contain elements that could be applied Stateside. Reverence for natural objects, beautifully mutilated or otherwise transformed by nature, was a novel idea to the Americans, who thereafter became fascinated by driftwood and weathered rocks. Calligraphy, especially when executed in a heavily inked, free manner, was also fresh and intriguing.

Quite distinctive work arose from these diverse influences and led to the publication of many prints in what was then considered an imaginative and original movement. In 1952 Rio Grande Graphics, "dedicated to the advancement of fine arts in the graphic field," began to issue portfolios of woodcuts and intaglio prints in editions of two hundred twenty-five. The series was publicized as an opportunity to have "your own 'museum without walls'" (Malraux's influential thesis had been published in 1948). Collecting prints became identified with collecting art, and significantly marked the end of an era in which print buyers had preferred familiar and referential imagery with which they could find some personal association. In 1975

Sylvan Cole, then director of Associated American Artists, which had been publishing prints since the 1930s, recalled, "By the early fifties the modern movement had taken a very thorough hold in America, and the American scene died overnight in the fastest death I could ever recall."[10]

In those infant years of modernist expression in prints, there remained a preference for figurative work. There was still a strong tendency toward the illustrative composition, incorporating an isolated subject without too much interference from additional or secondary images. Single figures, portraits, and animals were the dominant imagery in what seemed to be the most easily accessible contemporary works. In the fifties, the color prints of Antonio Frasconi and the mammoth expressionist woodcuts of Leonard Baskin represented the two important solutions in this area of printmaking. Both artists spent much of their creative time on book design and illustration, so it is not surprising that their single prints should have similarities with the current modes of book illustration. In a print such as *Monterey Fisherman* (1951, Fig. 23), Frasconi presents a diptych that is nearly the equivalent of a double-page spread. It is not impossible to imagine text superimposed upon the area of bay water to the right of the isolated figure. Frasconi often re-used blocks in other compositions and other formats. He continued to produce some of the very finest examples of the illustrative woodcut throughout the 1960s and '70s, adding to his extensive repertoire of images portraits of the martyrs of the civil rights movement and other Americans whose lives had heightened meaning in years that seemed filled with incursions upon "inalienable rights."

During his early career Leonard Baskin, like many of his generation, felt the injustices and disappointments of the post-war period very strongly (Fig. 24). To the group of works responding to the Korean conflict (*Man of Peace,* 1952) and the threat of "the bomb" (*Hydrogen Man,* 1954), he added a few religious subjects (*Angel of Death,* 1959, and *Haman,* 1955). These woodcuts, printed in mournful black from large plywood planks on Japanese shoji-screen paper, were powerful metaphors which, like much of the sculpture of the time, were meant to be political monuments. They communicated their message directly to the spectator through radical distortion of the human form and extreme scale. The figures were filled with webs of lines. Their outlines and mass derive from Baskin's sculpture, which also was often made of wood and revealed the irregular linear patterns of the grain.

The work of Ben Shahn, a dominant social painter of the 1930s, has already been mentioned. The silkscreens that he made beginning in 1941 were only occasionally evocative of his current style of painting; most of his illustrative prints were merely black drawings translated into silkscreen and hand-colored. Pre-war subjects, such as his bitter portrait *Sacco and Vanzetti* (1931–32, but redrawn in 1952), were issued as prints at moments when they would have the most meaningful public impact. For the most part, Shahn's new post-war images were less pointedly political and more decorative; however, subjects in such works as *Lute and Molecules* and *Scientist* (Fig. 25) allude to the changed situation in America as he perceived it. In 1959 Shahn wrote, "I doubt that what now seems to be an atomic age, or is in any case a scientifico-mechanical age, will ever be greatly distinguished for its contribution to the human spirit."[11]

Few of the works seen in "Modern Art in the United States" were geometric abstractions, a reflection of the displacement of 1930s-style abstraction by more emotionally impelled composition. Among the prints, only those by Albers and Ralston Crawford harkened back to the more precise and classical abstract style, while in the painting section the works of Fritz Glarner, I. Rice Pereira, and Atillio Salemme upheld that tradition in the face of the overwhelming excitement of Abstract Expressionist canvases. Crawford's work typifies the American abstractionist work of the 1930s as it attempted to maintain itself after the war. His color lithographs are based upon objects, but are much more simplified than the more powerful early-1930s prints of Stuart Davis, to which they owe a great deal. Crawford's wartime job, making some of the first weather maps, influenced his art very little. In his *Third Avenue El, No. 1* of 1952 (Fig. 26), the fresh contrasts of unmodulated bands of black and yellow give a premonition of one of the following decade's approaches to graphics.

Glarner, who conscientiously carried on Mondrian's systematic method, did what the master of De Stijl never managed: he made some prints. The Swiss painter, who arrived in America in 1936, was the second artist to work at Universal Limited Art Editions (ULAE), the lithography workshop that opened on Long Island in 1957. In 1958 Glarner began to draw his geometric sketches, usually plans for his *Relational Paintings,* on lithographic stones (Fig. 28). While other European artists of his generation were busily making lithographs and silkscreens in color that imitated their paintings as closely as possible, Glarner chose to expand our understanding of his immaculately finished paintings by making prints that divulged something of his creative process. That this was his intention is clear from the series of lithographic drawings recapitulating his important compositions in other mediums, which formed his book *Recollections* (ULAE, 1964–68).

Salemme, Pereira, and nineteen other artists, American and European, participated in a unique project begun at Atelier 17 in 1951, after Hayter's return to Paris. For the album *21 Etchings and Poems,* Peter Grippe, director of the workshop, brought together poets, whose handwritten verses were transferred to the plates, and artists, who provided the texts with illustrative borders. In 1960, after years of preparation without money or patronage, these etched broadside prints were compiled as an album by one of the poets, Morris Weisenthal, who distributed them through his gallery. The roster of poets and artists in the album is impressive, but the plates by Franz Kline and Willem de Kooning, two of the most important painters of the New York School, are particularly notable as being their first prints.

Of the other painters represented in "Modern Art in the United States," Grace Hartigan, a young Abstract Expressionist, also created a few prints at ULAE between 1960 and 1962 (Fig. 29). Clyfford Still had actually made at least one attempt at lithography in 1944, but no prints are known that reflect his mature style. The abstract painters Philip Guston, Willem de Kooning, Robert Motherwell, and Mark Tobey all made prints in the 1960s and '70s. Tobey, who left America to live abroad in 1960, executed all his prints in Europe. Beginning in 1961 at the age of seventy-one, he produced thirty lithographs before turning to aquatint in the 1970s. Nearly all of his prints depend upon lyrically deft and repetitive brush marks that animate the entire surface (Fig. 31).

Missing from "Modern Art in the United States" were the sculptures of David Smith, who had been included in "12 Contemporary American Painters and Sculptors," mounted in Paris by the Museum of Modern Art in 1953, but was inexplicably excluded from the more comprehensive selection a year later. His welded sculptures of the early 1950s incorporated much of the spirit of the new painting. He had made etchings in the 1930s, and had even worked in Hayter's Atelier 17 in Paris, but his interest in printmaking was only intermittent. Because, as we have seen, most painters and sculptors did not put much thought into the distribution of their prints at this time (the market for contemporary prints, where it existed at all, belonged to the printmakers), it is unlikely that anyone other than his friends would have paid attention to Smith's prints, even though one was included in an exhibition at the Metropolitan Museum of Art in 1952. His few black and white lithographs of the 1950s are quintessentially expressionist, with their sweeping strokes hinting at figurative elements and linking them together into structures not unlike his sculpture of the period (Fig. 27). Some were printed on the press of Margaret Loewengrund, who introduced many artists to lithography during this time and was instrumental in the founding of the Pratt Graphic Art Center. Smith's practice of making hundreds of drawings in brush and Oriental ink formed the basis of his lithographic style and forecast the manner of printmaking that many of the abstract painters would pursue some years later.

Lithography was not an utterly dead technique in America in the 1950s. As we have seen, a few artists who had been accustomed to the medium continued to work with it. However, such work on the East Coast suffered from the dominance of Hayter's workshop and from the attention to woodcuts that went together with a more individual attitude toward art manufacture. On the West Coast the artists who worked in the lithography shop of Lynton Kistler apparently had a much more satisfactory experience, enjoying the collaborative aspect of printmaking that is inherent in lithography. By and large, the artists who worked with Kistler were figurative in their point of view, Rico LeBrun being one of the most prominent painters in this style. Having settled in California in 1937, after more than a decade as a practicing commercial artist in New York, LeBrun continued the line of social realism that later underwent a Surrealist transformation. He made several prints in the 1940s and '50s, but his most ambitious work in lithography was done after the establishment of the Tamarind Lithography Workshop by June Wayne in 1960. There he created *Grünewald Study* (1961, Fig. 33), a moving image of his transcription of the famous Crucifixion on the Isenheim altarpiece.

June Wayne, a painter from Chicago, was another lithographer who learned from Kistler, finally seeking out more technically expert help in France after Kistler's death. Her prints of the 1950s wrestled with figurative elements that she abstracted with prisms or with atmospheric incursions such as clouds and waves (Fig. 32). She was the only dedicated lithographer in the "Modern Art" exhibition; her devotion to the medium prompted her to find a way to provide possibilities for other painters to try their hand at it. Her success in convincing the Ford Foundation to fund her Tamarind Lithography Workshop in Los Angeles for a decade (1960–70) led to a significant change in the way artists approach printmaking.

Wayne wished primarily to establish a base for the institution of lithographic workshops throughout the United States, by training printers. Recognizing that artists are the most demanding teachers, requiring solutions to problems that appear only during the actual process of making art, she and her colleagues Clinton Adams and Garo Antreasian began the workshop program by giving painters and sculptors two-month fellowships to live in Los Angeles and work at Tamarind with apprentice printers drawn from college art schools. Their compositions, drawn and painted on lithographic stones and plates, provided the materials with which the education of the printers could occur. A good deal of research into inks, papers, and plate materials was done at Tamarind during the decade of its existence, and many printers who were trained there later opened their own workshops across the country.

More than a hundred artists worked at Tamarind on the two-month grants, coming from many parts of the world, often with no printmaking experience. Because the work was concentrated into a finite period, and because there was no organized distribution of the editions produced, most of the nearly three thousand prints executed at Tamarind are little known. Wayne attempted to attract publicity for the prints by organizing museum exhibitions and by experimenting with new methods of distribution. She also conducted a study meant to show how to manage a successful art gallery that included prints in its inventory, based on the hypothetical "Blue Gallery"—actually a thin disguise for the Martha Jackson Gallery, probably the only one in New York that commissioned and sold prints in the early 1960s.

Many of the people who came to Tamarind were artists whose careers were bound to the West Coast. Few major painters found the time or interest to participate (and were often discouraged from doing so by their dealers), but many mature artists who had the incentive made dozens of fine lithographs there. Rico LeBrun, other figurative painters such as Leon Golub, James McGarrell, and Nathan Oliveira, and quite a few representational printmakers worked at Tamarind in the early years. Richard Diebenkorn, who in the 1970s and '80s made abstract prints derived from landscape subjects, created several figurative prints at Tamarind in 1965.

The traditional depiction of the human figure was nearly obliterated by the harsh confrontation with Pop Art during the 1960s, but there was one artist, Larry Rivers, for whom the figure continued to be a central means of representing a view of life that was less respectful but more pertinent to the new reality. (New Realism was the French version of the melange of contradictory popular and Neo-Dadaist representations that preceded the advent of Pop Art.) He was the one painter who consistently carried through the underlying remnants of figuration that only occasionally rose to prominence in works of de Kooning and others in the Abstract Expressionist movement. In 1957, when Rivers's friends Tatyana and Maurice Grosman asked the painter if he would like to make a book of some sort, working on lithographic stones, he was willing to experiment.

Tatyana Grosman was a newspaper publisher's daughter, born in Siberia and educated at the Dresden Academy of Arts and Crafts. Never a practicing artist nor a businesswoman, she was forced to find a means of supporting herself and her artist husband after his heart attack made it impossible for him to continue painting, teaching, and making silkscreen reproductions of famous modern works. In their cottage in West Islip, Long Island, an hour's drive from New York City, Mrs. Grosman bravely started an enterprise for which her only preparation was patience, persistence, and taste. With a secondhand lithographic press, some lithographic stones found in her garden, and the encouragement of Maurice's students and artist acquaintances, Universal Limited Art Editions was launched in 1957.

Rivers, the first artist to work at ULAE, began his book project by drawing sketchy renderings of momentary impressions on a few of the small stones. Portraits of his wife Clarisse, compositions with birds, and other instantaneous peeps at objects were the subjects of his first attempts. Simultaneously he began to work directly on stones with the poet Frank O'Hara, the latter writing a line or two in response to the image drawn by Rivers, or vice versa, until a poem or poetic idea was completed. A dozen lithographs, so composed, were printed and housed inside a folder made of heavy blue paper manufactured from blue-jeans fabric, to form the unconventional book *Stones* (1957–59). Rivers's irreverent representation of real people and objects verged upon the emerging movement that was known as Pop Art (Fig. 35). But however much commercial and advertising imagery he included in his work, he never abandoned the representation of reality. In his paintings and prints of the 1950s he presented a revised view of the (new) world. Because his images seem to fade or have few areas where the eye can accurately distinguish more than small details, Rivers's work hovers between expressionism and a form of Impressionism in which reality is perceived as a fleeting image, much as it exists on television.

1. Stanley William Hayter. *Tarantella*. 1943.
Engraving and etching,
21¹¹/₁₆ x 13″ (55.0 x 32.9 cm.)

2. Jackson Pollock. Untitled 1. 1944. Engraving and drypoint, 11⅝ x 9¹⁵/₁₆″ (29.5 x 25.3 cm.). The Museum of
Modern Art, New York, gift of Lee Krasner Pollock

3. Jackson Pollock. Untitled 4. 1945. Engraving and drypoint, 14¾ x 17⅞″ (37.5 x 45.4 cm.). The Museum of Modern Art, New York, gift of Lee Krasner Pollock

About a decade after the death of Jackson Pollock, a search through his works stored in a warehouse revealed some metal plates and a stack of printed trial proofs of the engravings he had made at Atelier 17 in 1944–45. This example, one of two larger prints made in 1945, shows the energy and plethora of details, annotations, and sweeping rhythms that Pollock was able to put into his works at this vital moment. The pervasive influence is that of Picasso, whose bullfight compositions of 1935 seem to have been plagiarized to a degree. The structure of one Picasso print, for example, includes a spectator to the right and a woman bullfighter thrown over the back of her horse in the center, creating a maelstrom of activity. Similarly, Pollock has used the bracketing viewer, now on the left, and heaving, hysterical movement in the center. Strewn through-

out the composition are the arrows, fish, and other mystical signs that inhabited many of the paintings of the time as artists drew symbolism from sources in Greek mythology. This work also derives from Hayter's advocacy of the use of automatism; the sweeping lines emanating from the left suggest Poseidon throwing out his net. The subject, if one can call it that, is a point of departure for the organization of an abstract composition. In such all-over patterning, one sees the harbinger of Pollock's impending liberation from the rigid rules of composition, in which beginnings, ends, tops, and bottoms counted for more than the picture plane itself.

In 1967, after this and six other plates (with a total of eight engraved sides) were discovered, editions of fifty were printed of seven of the engravings, following as closely as possible the last proofs. Thus, during the golden age of American printmaking, Pollock's unique contribution entered the cultural consciousness.

4. Kurt Seligmann. *Acteon*. 1947. Etching, 11¾ x 8¹³⁄₁₆″ (30.2 x 22.4 cm.)

5. Robert Motherwell. *Personnage*. 1944. Engraving with salt-lift ground, 11⁹⁄₁₆ x 7¹⁵⁄₁₆″ (29.4 x 20.1 cm). Metropolitan Museum of Art, New York, Stewart S. McDermott Fund, 1974

6. Adolph Gottlieb. *Apparition* (ca. 1945). Aquatint and drypoint, 20⅛ x 15⅛″ (51.1 x 38.4 cm.). Adolph and Esther Gottlieb Foundation, Inc.

This, the largest of Adolph Gottlieb's intaglio prints of the 1940s, is typical of the pictographic style he practiced between 1941 and 1952. The irregular squares and rectangles containing primitive symbols and figures derived from real and imaginary sources are massed together to form an even more substantial symbolic image. He gave his paintings of this period titles such as *Masquerade*, *Dream*, and *Recurrent Apparition*, indicating their origin in the subconscious or in the mysterious territory of primitive culture. The setting of individual images within a grid structure had interested abstract artists for some time, dominating the work of the Uruguayan Joaquin Torres-García, which was shown together with other Latin American art in New York during the war. Gottlieb was not concerned with the Constructivist theory that governed Torres-García's compositions of folk signs, but he too sought a method of expressing the magic of his chosen symbols within an organized space. Ultimately, only the symbols, refined and divested of figurative elements, remained in his works. During the time that Gottlieb created his pictographs he was able to put in graphic form the sketchy, shorthand markings that signaled his progression toward complete abstract expression.

7. Mauricio Lasansky. *Eye for an Eye IV.*
1946–48. Etching and engraving,
26⅜ x 21¹⁄₁₆″ (67.0 x 53.6 cm.). University of Iowa Museum of Art, gift of Dr.
and Mrs. Webster B. Gelman

8. Gabor Peterdi. *Germination.*
1952. Aquatint, etching, and engraving, 19¾ x 23¹³⁄₁₆″
(50.0 x 60.5 cm.). The Museum
of Modern Art, New York, gift
of Mr. and Mrs. Walter Bareiss

9. Max Beckmann. *King and Demagogue* from the portfolio *Day and Dream*. (1946). Published by Curt Valentin. Transfer lithograph, 14⅞ x 10″ (37.8 x 25.4 cm.). Courtesy of Associated American Artists

In his last series of prints, made from ink drawings that had been sent from Europe some months before his arrival in America, Max Beckmann recapitulated several themes that had appeared in his paintings since the 1930s. He had spent most of the war drawing and painting in Holland, and had delved even more deeply than before into the imaginary world from which he retrieved a large variety of characters. His interest in Greek mythology emerges often, as kings make their epic journeys in and out of contemporary scenes of bored models and wastepaper. This extremely personal,

metaphorical expression was vital in a period when the creative imagination was being repressed in Europe. In this print the king sits nonchalantly, rather weak in demeanor, while the female demagogue, behind her bearded mask, holds a paper and significantly points to it. In his allegorical painting of 1942, *The Actors*, the king (recognizably a portrait of Beckmann himself) stabs himself in front of a masked woman, while in an adjacent panel a person quietly reads *The New York Times*. Now, after the war, it is the masked lady who reminds the king of "Time." Elsewhere in the portfolio is a self-portrait uncomplicated by the symbols and strange conjunctions of the other prints. The title of the portfolio thus reflects Beckmann's basic concern with the outer and inner realms of reality.

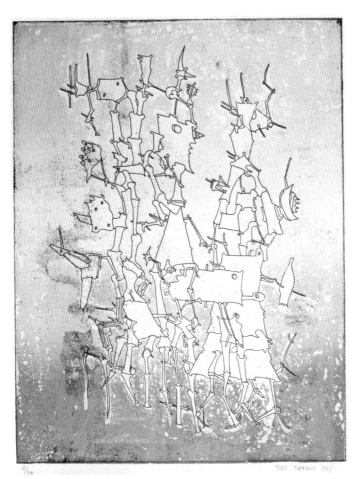

10. Yves Tanguy. *Rhabdomancie* from *Brunidor Portfolio No. 1*. 1947. Color etching, 11¹¹⁄₁₆ x 8¹³⁄₁₆″ (29.7 x 22.4 cm.)

11. Jacques Lipchitz. *Theseus*. ca. 1944. Etching, engraving, and aquatint, 13¹³⁄₁₆ x 11³⁄₁₆″ (35.1 x 28.4 cm.). Associated American Artists

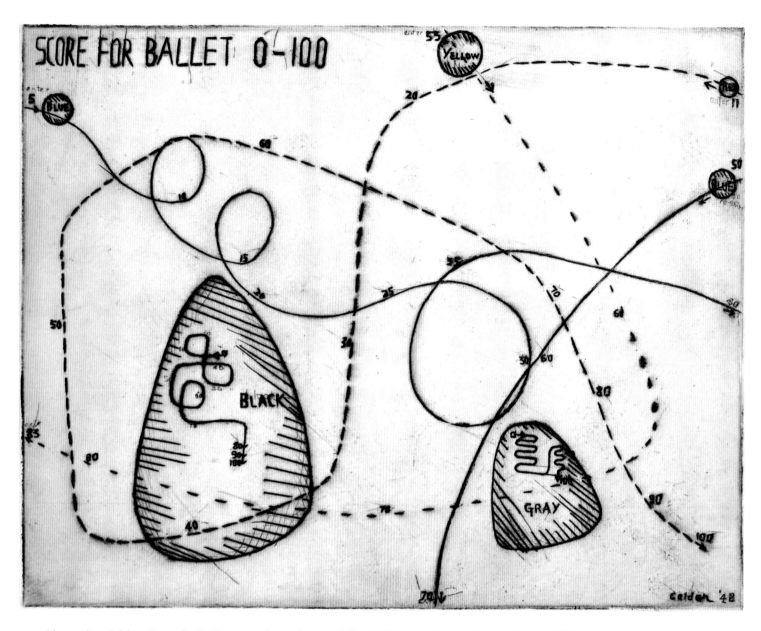

12. Alexander Calder. *Score for Ballet 0–100* from the portfolio *VVV.* 1942. Engraving, 11⅜ x 14⅞″ (28.9 x 37.8 cm.)

Plate 6   L. Bourgeois

13. Louise Bourgeois. Plate 6 from *He Disappeared into Complete Silence*. 1947. Engraving, 6¹³⁄₁₆ x 5⅜" (17.3 x 13.7 cm.)

In 1945, like many other younger artists who were attracted to the Surrealist idiom, Louise Bourgeois began to make prints at Atelier 17. Born and educated in France, Bourgeois was a friend of many European émigrés who often met together at the print studio. Her engravings at Atelier 17 signaled a profound change in her career, culminating in her definitive commitment to sculpture in 1949. During the mid-1940s, however, she shared with Adolph Gottlieb and other American artists the system of squaring off her compositions into grids. For her this evolved into a mystical, architectonic style. At first she created a group of paintings generally titled *Femme-Maison* (Woman-House), in which the heads or upper bodies were transformed into buildings. In 1947, at Atelier 17, she moved entirely away from the figure in her book of nine engravings, *He Disappeared into Complete Silence*, presenting instead all manner of construction images, including columns, sheds, and ladders. The accompanying text is full of human imagery, usually in the form of parables or moral tales. Some stories refer to the engravings facing them—for example, opposite a columnar object Bourgeois writes, ". . . the purpose of this picture is to show how beautiful she was." These prints represent one of the Surrealist derivations independent of automatic drawing, which had been Hayter's preferred method of fathoming the subconscious.

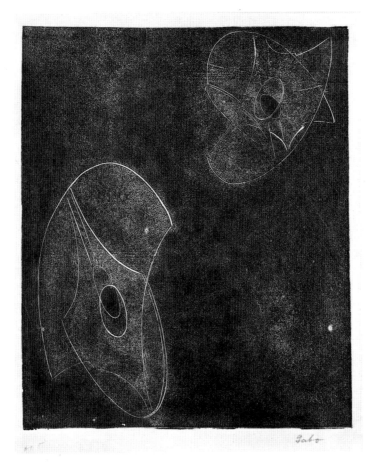

14. Naum Gabo. *Opus* 5 ("Constellations"). 1951. Wood-engraving monoprint, 9½ x 8″ (24.1 x 20.3 cm.). Museum of Fine Arts, Boston, Lee M. Friedman Fund

After years of moving from country to country since he left Russia in 1922, the sculptor Naum Gabo arrived in America in 1946. He began a very personal project in 1950, cutting a series of wood engravings which he inked and printed in many different ways. The variety of printings has led them to be classified as monoprints, even though the basic linear image cut into each block is necessarily consistent. Gabo carefully manipulated the ink on the block's surface, seeking the texture, degree of transparency and opacity, and color that would give the shapes defined by the unprinted white lines their balance and spatial position. Like his clear glass and plastic sculptures that, mirage-like, float in and out of a distinct site, the placement of Gabo's curvilinear shapes has a similar transient reference to space. Printed on thin Japanese paper given to him by his neighbor, the woodcut artist Claire Leighton, *Opus* 5 was subtitled "Constellations" because Gabo saw in his printing an allusion to the Milky Way. Gabo continued his career as a sculptor in America, producing work that was based on the Constructivist theories he brought from Russia, and he had several public exhibitions before his death in 1977. He made prints until 1973, but these were not exhibited, remaining a purely private enterprise. Nevertheless, he gave away individual examples over the years and these were, like many of the early prints of painters and sculptors in America, considered mainly tokens of friendship.

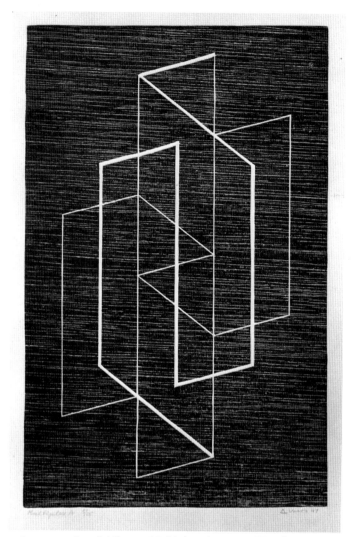

16. ABOVE Josef Albers. *Multiplex A*. 1947. Woodcut,
11¹⁵/₁₆ x 7¹⁵/₁₆″ (30.3 x 20.1 cm.). Brooke Alexander, Inc.

15. LEFT Josef Albers. *Ascension* from *Graphic Tectonic*. 1942.
Offset lithograph, 17³/₁₆ x 8⅛″ (43.7 x 20.7 cm.)

17. Louis Schanker. *Static and Revolving*. 1945.
Woodcut, 14⅜ x 21⅛″ (36.5 x 53.7 cm.). New
York Public Library

18. Adja Yunkers. *Miss Ever-Ready* from *Rio
Grande Graphics*. 1952. Published by Ted Gotthelf.
Woodcut, 18⅜ x 9⅝″ (46.9 x 24.5 cm.). The Mu-
seum of Modern Art, New York, purchase

19. Carol Summers. *Chinese Landscape*. 1951. Woodcut, 21³⁄₁₆ x 36" (53.8 x 91.4 cm.). The Museum of Modern Art, New York, gift of Mr. Donald B. Straus

In his earliest post-war woodcuts, Carol Summers, a student of Louis Schanker, reviewed several of the traditional applications and styles of the medium. His own individual technique is only beginning to develop in this decorative work. Conscious of the Oriental artist's sensitivity to materials, Summers emphasizes the dominating grain of the wood while outlining the hill formations with fluid calligraphic strokes. Strong, opaque color creates a vivid contrast with the

fragile Oriental paper. In later prints Summers utilized a form of "resist" technique in which a printed area of opaque white resists the subsequent application of color. One of the very first artists to understand the properties of paper (especially the Japanese types that woodcut artists prefer), he quite often printed on both front and back of the sheet, sometimes staining the paper over woodblock forms instead of inking and printing directly from the wood. Such printing could not have been done without firsthand experience of Japanese techniques and an appreciation of the reverence Japanese artisans have for their materials.

20. Adolph Gottlieb. Untitled. Ca. 1945. Color woodcut, 14¹³⁄₁₆ x 11¹³⁄₁₆" (37.6 x 30.0 cm.). New York Public Library

21. Milton Avery. *Dancer.* 1954. Woodcut, 12¹⁄₁₆ x 9¹¹⁄₁₆" (30.6 x 24.6 cm.). Associated American Artists

Already in his fifties during World War II, Milton Avery had persisted in depicting the New England landscape of his youth in the most acceptable American modernist style. His forms became broader with fewer details as color shapes defined his subjects, whether human or landscape. In his paintings Avery showed his considerable indebtedness to Matisse, both in palette and composition. His series of drypoints of the 1930s attempted, too, to capture the quality of the French master's spontaneously fluent line without sacrificing his own disingenuousness. While these early works seem somewhat feeble in expression, Avery's woodcuts have the spontaneity that appears essential to both his subjects (birds, women, and seascapes) and their arrangement. In 1950, recovering from a heart attack in Florida, he had begun to make monotypes under the guidance of the printmaker Boris Margo. Feeling stronger in 1952, he began to make woodcuts, as many of his artist colleagues were doing. The woodcuts are simple, direct statements, often quite decorative with their repetitive images. The graceful humor of this dancer, whose few facial features and precarious balance animate the scratchy composition, corresponds to the general sense of gentle peace that pervades Avery's work.

22. Antonio Frasconi. *Monterey Fisherman*. 1951. Woodcut on two sheets, 19½ x 33⁵⁄₁₆″ (49.5 x 84.1 cm.). The Museum of Modern Art, New York, Inter-American Fund

23. Misch Kohn. *Season in Hell*. 1951. Wood engraving, 19 x 28⁹⁄₁₆″ (48.3 x 72.5 cm.). New York Public Library

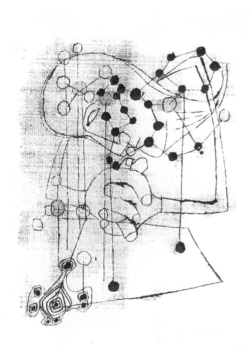

24. Ben Shahn. *Scientist*. 1957. Serigraph, hand-colored, 8¾ x 6¹⁵⁄₁₆″ (22.2 x 17.6 cm.). New Jersey State Museum Collection, Trenton, Museum Purchase

25. Leonard Baskin. *Torment*. 1958. Woodcut, 31 x 23⁵⁄₁₆″ (78.6 x 59.2 cm.)

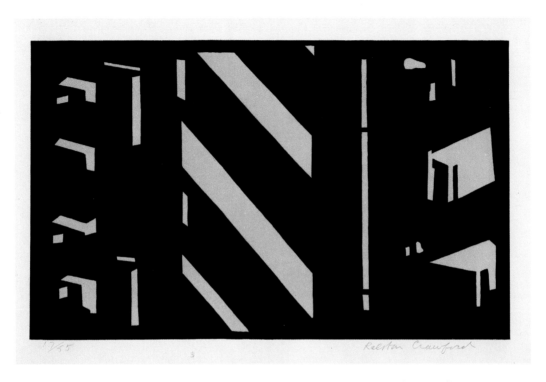

26. Ralston Crawford. *Third Avenue El, No. 1*. 1952. Lithograph, 10⅜ x 17⅜″ (26.4 x 44.1 cm.). The Museum of Modern Art, New York, Abby Aldrich Rockefeller Fund

27. David Smith. *Composition.* 1954. Lithograph, 8⁹⁄₁₆ x 22¾″ (21.8 x 57.8 cm.). The Museum of Modern Art, New York, Mrs. John D. Rockefeller 3rd Fund

28. Fritz Glarner. *Drawing for Tondo*. 1959. Published by Universal Limited Art Editions. Lithograph, 14⁵⁄₁₆ x 13¹⁵⁄₁₆″ (36.3 x 35.0 cm.)

29. Grace Hartigan. *The Ship*. 1960. Published by Universal Limited Art Editions. Lithograph, 12⅞ x 16⅜″ (32.7 x 41.6 cm.)

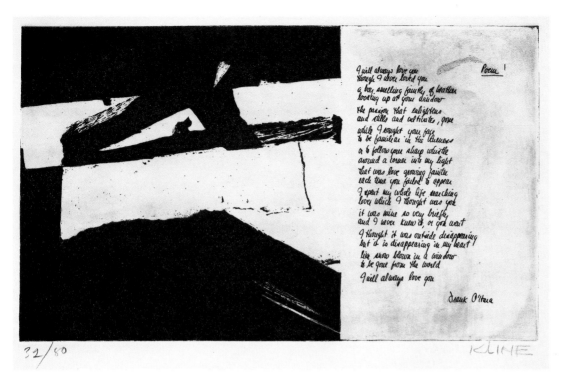

30. Franz Kline. *Poem* by Frank O'Hara from *21 Etchings and Poems*. 1960. Published by Morris Gallery. Etching and photoengraving, 8⁷⁄₁₆ x 14⁷⁄₁₆″ (21.7 x 37.0 cm.)

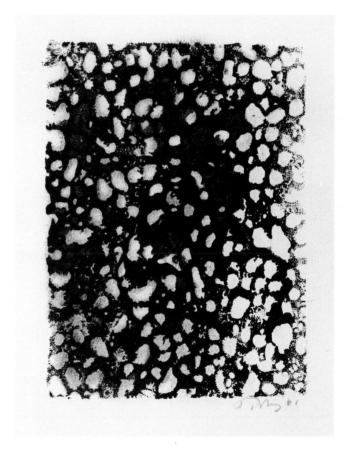

31. Mark Tobey. *Winter*. 1961. Published by Galerie Beyeler, Basel. Color lithograph, 4¹⁵⁄₁₆ x 3⁵⁄₈″ (12.5 x 9.2 cm.). Courtesy David Anderson Gallery

32. June Wayne. *The Travellers.* 1954. Lithograph, 25¼ x 18½"
(64.1 x 47.0 cm.)

33. Rico Lebrun. *Grünewald Study.* 1961. Lithograph,
25⁹⁄₁₆ x 30⁷⁄₁₆" (65.5 x 77.3 cm.)

34. James McGarrell. *Portland I*. 1962. Lithograph, 35¼ x 25⅜″ (89.5 x 64.5 cm.).
The Museum of Modern Art, New York, gift of Kleiner, Bell and Co.

1/20   I   *Rivers '61*

35. Larry Rivers. *Last Civil War Veteran I*. 1961. Published by Universal Limited Art Editions. Lithograph, 17½ x 12⅝″ (44.5 x 32.1 cm.)

In 1960 *Life* magazine reproduced a photograph of the last veteran of the Civil War, Walter Williams, as he lay in his coffin, surrounded by an honor guard and wreaths of flowers. Larry Rivers used this image as the basis for several paintings that year, one of the most abstract renderings titled *The Final Veteran*. Two versions of the subject, one in color, were made into lithographs, following a habit Rivers began with his first attempts in the medium. Prominent in the image is the recognizable diagonal crossing of the Confederate flag that draped the coffin. The strong pattern organizes the unstable, dashed-off marks that lightly refer to the specific subject. Rivers seems to have appreciated the manner in which flags, uniforms, and other military accoutrements identified and classified society, and he used them with a certain amount of mockery in the 1950s in his famous painting based on the popular pseudo-historic tableau *George Washington Crossing the Delaware*. Rarely going beyond figuration, he has nevertheless often selected the inherent organizing patterns that abstract the literal and topical suggestions of his work from advertisements, commemorative photographs, and other conventionalized graphic forms.

CHAPTER THREE

In reaction to the extravagantly subjective criticism that illuminated the work of the Abstract Expressionists with a parallel mystical language, it became customary to surround the explanation of the development of art into the 1960s with a scaffold of socio-economic buttressing. The history of art in the form of prints has been more often a history of the organizations that produced the prints than a study of the works themselves. Certainly, the involvement of business people offered possibilities for a massive production of prints, and there were several who provided spiritual as well as material encouragement to artists whose subsequent work in all mediums benefited profoundly from such support. The development of the workshop-publisher complex in America in the 1960s cannot be dissociated from the quality of the art produced within it, even though art, rather than the circumstances of its creation, is all that tends to remain memorable. Nevertheless, the preferences of publishers and workshop directors, like those of art dealers, have limited the number of artists and the sort of artistic styles or expressions that have been represented. The study of the prints of Jasper Johns, Robert Rauschenberg, and other masters of the 1960s, therefore, is incomprehensible without reference to the commercial complex that had already determined the kinds of art that might survive into the future.

Proportionately more interest in prints had been evinced by the public during the fifteen years after the war than before it; this can be attributed to increasing affluence and a higher level of education that led to increased participation in cultural activities such as art classes and museum attendance. Still, in those years the prints preferred by the American public were by famous European painters such as Picasso and Chagall, or were the type issued by printmakers. Numerous exhibitions brought the latter to the attention of this public and, through their inclusion in surveys of American art that traveled abroad, of Europeans, too. It is quite possible that, had the major Abstract Expressionists been making prints as well as paintings during the 1950s, their prints would not have been included in such showings, since a double standard seemed to prevail: Picasso and Chagall could and did create prints with the same subjects and compositions as their paintings, and this was acceptable, but when American painters began to do the same (Jasper Johns's *Flag,* for example), they were said to be making reproductions. A warped standard which could only be characterized as fundamental American puritanism was applied to printmaking, and was strictly formalized in the proceedings of the Print Council of America. This body was established in 1956 by the collector Lessing Rosenwald and a group of curators as a forum for the discussion of prints and the protection of the print buyer from misrepresentations of originality. The challenge of overcoming this perceived inequity might at least partly explain the subsequent flourishing of printmaking among painters and sculptors.

The announcement of a set of rules for originality in printmaking coincided with the establishment of the Pratt Graphic Art Center in New York in 1956. It was planned as a workshop for teaching printmaking techniques to students, but it was also hoped that mature painters would come to try their hands at the various print mediums. The aim was really no different from that expressed by the Print Council, for Pratt wanted artists to work directly on plates and stones rather than allow their work to be "reproduced" by craftsmen. The Print Council had reacted to a widespread European practice of having *chromistes* copy onto lithographic stones the watercolor, gouache, or even oil compositions of well-known painters and represent these prints as originals. This practice was confusing if not abhorrent to traditionally skeptical Americans, and every possible means of encouraging American artists to avoid it was explored. The Rockefeller Foundation provided the impetus for the Pratt Center, the Ford Foundation funded the Tamarind Lithography Workshop in Los Angeles in 1960, and other means (encouraging hand processes over photographic ones, for example) kept the creation of prints within these guidelines.

With this burgeoning of organization it is not surprising that in 1960 and 1961 several Abstract Expressionists finally made lithographs (de Kooning, Motherwell, and Barnett Newman) and the most important artist-printmaker of the ensuing two decades (Jasper Johns) began this aspect of his career. In the unusual circumstance of the Abstract Expressionists finally making prints, it should be noted that not one of them actively sought the opportunity to do so. Both de Kooning and Newman, however, had been making drawings of a type so eminently adaptable to lithography that, when other artists suggested to them that they go into a workshop and draw on a lithographic stone, they were prepared and able to do so, and do so well.

De Kooning's large, dashingly brushed collage drawings of 1960 were executed in a free and immediate fashion that he applied to the problem of drawing on stone. One evening two artist-printmakers, Nathan Oliveira and George Miyasake, brought him to their workshop at the University of California in Berkeley. There he saw a very large stone just waiting for someone to place a very large image upon it, and that is exactly what de Kooning did, twice, with a floor mop dipped into tusche. According to witnesses, the painter stood on the surface where the stone lay and drew as if he were swabbing the decks! Whatever his method, the sure movements of the "action" painter were transferred to the stone, instantly printed by his friends in only a few copies, and that inimitable American bravado that characterized Abstract Expressionism was captured in print for the first time (Fig. 36).

While de Kooning's first prints were the products of an exhilarating communal experience, Barnett Newman was brought to the Pratt Graphic Art Center for therapeutic reasons. Mourning the recent death of his brother, Newman had not painted for a few months. A friend, the painter Cleve Gray, thought that trying to work in a new medium might occupy Newman's mind and get him back to thinking about his painting. As with de Kooning, Newman had spent some time drawing in black and white before he was led to attempt a lithograph. There were enough similarities to give the artist a certain amount of confidence in working with tusche on some small stones, both at the workshop and at home. The first of the three prints he did at Pratt mimicked the small scale of his 1960 drawings, mostly on 14-by-10-inch sheets of paper, but Newman exhibited considerable natural ability in managing the materials of lithography.

After these preliminary efforts, Newman, unlike any of the other older Abstract Expressionists at the time, made an effort to execute a major work in lithography. His album *18 Cantos,* produced at ULAE in 1963–64, was a set of variations exploiting color, proportion, and other formal elements that he had developed in his paintings. A single vertical element, or "zip," sliced into an unmodulated rectangular field of color or interrupted that same field as a vertical textured band (Fig. 39). *18 Cantos* was an intense creative experience for this most intellectual member of the New York School. He began with the idea of a small suite of prints, but eventually, captivated by the ways in which printing could alter color appearances, increased the total to eighteen compositions.

Newman, however, cannot be seen as a typical Abstract Expressionist, since the idea of "action painting" is not central to his work as it is to the art of de Kooning, Motherwell, and Gottlieb. De Kooning returned to printmaking for brief periods in 1967 and 1970 when he befriended a former Tamarind printer, Irwin Hollander, who had opened a workshop in New York. Hollander had worked with Motherwell in 1965 and hoped (as many other printers had) that de Kooning, his famous neighbor on Tenth Street, would want to try his hand at lithography once again. The twenty black and white lithographs that resulted from de Kooning's 1970 project are replete with flowing, brushy lines, some made to seem even more Oriental by being printed on translucent Japanese paper. At this time de Kooning had returned to more figurative forms, and most of the prints represent, in rather obscurely abstract ways, landscapes and people (Fig. 37). An attempt to equate the printed surface with an ink drawing (most of the prints were transfer lithographs) lessened the vitality of most of these prints, and the relatively short-lived collaboration was never revived. Thereafter, de Kooning has rarely made prints, only occasionally producing a collage or gouache for reproduction in silkscreen. The studio was his creative home.

Adolph Gottlieb was represented by Marlborough Fine Arts Gallery, whose print division was eager to have some of its American artists add to the bins of British prints already in stock. In most cases Gottlieb merely reworked the compositions of his paintings in a print medium (usually silkscreen). The harsh calligraphic markings of his paintings are rarely animated by an equivalent spirit in his prints (Fig. 41). He occasionally worked in lithography, which allowed him to be more autographic, and in the 1970s he made a few aquatints on his own press before a stroke enfeebled him.

In the early 1960s two important projects were undertaken which, like the workshops, were instrumental in introducing artists to the possibilities of printmaking. Arturo Schwarz, a Milanese art dealer and expert on Dada and Surrealism, produced a six-volume series, the overall title of which was *The International Avant Garde* (published 1962–64). These books gave a comprehensive representation, through small, souvenir-like etchings and drypoints, of many of the well-known and emerging painters and sculptors of the mid-twentieth century. The roster of a hundred artists (mostly Europeans) who contributed plates, often hastily scratched mementos of their familiar subjects and styles, is formidable. Most significant for the history of American printmaking, however, is the total absence of the Abstract Expressionists, whom Schwarz apparently did not consider to be part of the "avant-garde," and the participation of many members of the emerging Pop Art movement, chosen by Billy Kluver. Although Jasper Johns and Robert Rauschenberg, whose work had within it the seeds of Pop and who were possibly the most important artists at the time of the project, were also omitted, the volume titled *America Discovered* did include Jim Dine, Robert Indiana, Roy Lichtenstein, Claes Oldenburg (Fig. 42), James Rosenquist, and Andy Warhol (Fig. 43). Several of the etchings were made in 1962 at the Pratt Graphic Art Center workshop, where some of the artists had already tried their hand at other kinds of printmaking.★ As a compendium of attitudes toward artistic styles at the moment when art was about to become an extremely prominent subject in the American consciousness, Schwarz's little-known anthology is a vital document.

The other publication of importance to the subsequent blossoming of art in printed form was the project of two artists: Walasse Ting, a Chinese poet and painter who worked in Paris before coming to New York, and Sam Francis, who had met Ting in Paris in 1962. Unwittingly emulating Tatyana Grosman, whom he did not know, Ting carried materials for making lithographs around to his artist friends in Paris and New York, so that they could create full-page images for his poems in a book titled *1¢ Life*. For the most part, the European artists were former members of the COBRA movement then living in Paris. (The COBRA movement was a group of expressionist painters from Copenhagen, Brussels, and Amsterdam whose work paralleled in many ways that of the American Abstract Expressionists.) But in America Ting went to Rauschenberg and the Pop Artists—Dine, Indiana, Lichtenstein, Oldenburg, Warhol—although he also included the "action" painters Joan Mitchell, Kimber Smith, and Sam Francis. The only older American artist in *1¢ Life* is Alfred Jensen, a painter whose curious checkerboard compositions forecast by more than a decade the work of the Conceptualists.

1¢ Life, published in 1964, marks the first appearance of some of Pop Art's more cogent imagery as color prints. The brightly hued silkscreens and lithographs of the Pop Artists formed a memorable part of their creative production, and these early representations of what they felt appropriate to Ting's and Francis's project are clues to their attitudes toward both illustration and printmaking itself. For example, Warhol's lips of Marilyn Monroe, a repetitious image he had recently used on canvas, surround Ting's poem "Jade White Butterfly" like so many fluttering wings, enhancing Ting's own lyric image (Fig. 44). Lichtenstein's excerpted cartoon panel, *Fresh Air 1$25¢* (Fig. 45), interrupts the book with an out-of-context abruptness and, like Ting's often scatological verse, creates an exciting disjunction that intensifies the

---

★Dine and Oldenburg made lithographs at Pratt in 1960–61, and Dine also made about twenty drypoints there: a small portfolio of hand-colored objects and some enormous vertical plates with men's neckties scratched upon them which, with their exceptional scale, impassioned line but minimal detail, and hand-coloring, should perhaps be considered precursors of the kind of print propagated in the 1980s.

overall rhythm. Finally, one is aware of the attitude toward visual imagery that Ting wanted the book to convey. It is the lively, disingenuous vitality of the COBRA and Pop Artists that provides the new punctuation to our understanding of the ordinary. Ting, in his odd, pseudo-Oriental, brat manner, permitted the artists to reveal their intentions more insightfully than they could in a normal gallery exhibition of their paintings and constructions. This must certainly have further convinced many of them of printmaking's vast possibilities. With these two encouraging projects and the advent of the intrepid pioneering women—June Wayne, Tatyana Grosman, Rosa Esman, Marion Goodman, and others—whose workshops and publishing acumen offered painters and sculptors the chance to create and sell prints, the scene was set for undreamt-of developments.

A basic instinct of those who opened the first workshops was to entice the newly successful Abstract Expressionists to work in mediums that were new to them. A comparison of the Tamarind and ULAE approaches to painters reveals much about the resulting roster of artists at each. As we have seen, June Wayne's method was to offer artists two-month grants to come and collaborate with the printers at Tamarind. But accepting her invitation meant devoting two months to the creation of prints without any of the customary privacy of a studio. Any artist who did accept was either so attracted by the prospect of making prints that nothing was more important at the time, or was in no position to turn it (and the stipend) down—although those who had gallery representation were often discouraged by their dealers from spending time on prints.

ULAE's approach to an artist was often made by Tatyana Grosman herself, coming to deliver a few small lithographic stones to the artist's own studio. Some, Franz Kline for example, refused to touch them. Others, like Barnett Newman, were snared. The lithographic medium was a mystery to Robert Motherwell, whose only previous printmaking experience had been at Atelier 17 (Fig. 5). Although Tatyana Grosman had hoped that he would be one of the first artists to work with her, he did not come to West Islip until 1961, four years after the founding of ULAE. He has referred to his first experience there as "abortive." It is true that his first stone, made in two states, lacked the clarity and perfect spontaneity that he desired (and which was evident in his work in other mediums). His third print, *In Black with Yellow Ochre* (Fig. 38), produced a better effect, but it is clear, after studying his later prints, that Motherwell had not yet committed himself to printmaking.

Another "action" painter who was an early visitor to ULAE was Sam Francis, who began a few stones there in 1958. However, Francis left New York before completing even one print. His first lithographs were published in 1960 in Switzerland, having been printed in the workshop of Emil Matthieu, where Francis had been sent by a Swiss gallery to make a poster for his one-man show (Fig. 40). He made sixteen color lithographs in Switzerland, all executed in the method he evidently had begun to work out at ULAE. Each stone was drawn with some sense of the final composition but not, as is usual, painstakingly composed so that each separate color would fit exactly in a premeditated format. Francis would then have the stones proofed together, changing the order of printing, often changing the color combinations, and occasionally changing directions. Finally, the perfect combination of these variables was revealed and an edition printed. Francis, a Californian, later contributed a good deal of professional energy and example to the development of excellent printers at Tamarind. Both he and Motherwell eventually found printmaking to be a central means of expression and ultimately fit it into their studio life, acquiring presses and employing their own printers.

Aside from the individual prints that she helped to bring into existence, Tatyana Grosman's most significant achievement was undoubtedly her success in convincing artists of the highest caliber that printmaking was an activity that they should approach without distrust or fear. When she invited Jasper Johns to work at ULAE in 1960, he was in his thirtieth year, already associated with Leo Castelli's gallery, and had just had his work shown in a museum exhibition for the first time ("Sixteen Americans," Museum of Modern Art). His was, nevertheless, a new and distinctly discomforting style, with few links to the generally approved action painting of the previous decades. To Tatyana Grosman, Johns's art was at once perplexing and enchanting. His audacious compositions used the discernible, familiar forms of targets and American flags, subjects which, because of the viewer's already well-assimilated responses to abstract art, now were incorporated in a far more complex experience than mere recognition of the object. The combination of immediate recognition and the impact of an Abstract Expressionist texture contributed to a vertiginous aesthetic, intensely reflective of the way visual perception had been profoundly changed since the advent of instant telecommunication.

If the subject of art in the mid-twentieth century had become largely the process of its manufacture, set out without inference or objective connotation, then Johns's work had to be accepted on this basis. It was, understandably, exceedingly difficult to be confronted with an American flag, that instrument of knee-jerk national piety, and accept it merely as a vehicle for composing a picture, a means of presenting anew the process of creating a visual impression. In selecting his images with their abstract qualities, or, let us say, geometric structure, in mind, Johns had created a framework, albeit an overly familiar one, to support the collage, brushstroke, and crayon scribble that animated the surface. To emphasize that surface he also imprinted parts of his own body on the canvas, or attached plaster casts of body parts to it either directly or in cabinet-like boxes.

Johns's concern was to clarify the differences between art and image-making. He was perhaps the first to comprehend exactly how ambiguous visual information had become since the incursion of television and other mechanically created imagery. He played with this idea in works such as *False Start* and *Hatteras* (Fig. 48), in which he spelled out the names of colors on brushstroked or flat areas of color, some of which mischievously did not match their labels. The concept of misrepresentation, perhaps not yet consciously perceived as a basic cultural aberration of the period that began with the Korean conflict, is a subject that Jasper Johns has fully explored and exploited in his art.

Johns's first lithographs were small in scale: *Target* (1960) and *0 – 9* (1960–63), which consisted of ten prints, each with a different large numeral in the center and a frieze of all ten numbers above. At nearly the same time Johns attempted a much larger print, a sequential plotting of the alphabet, a pattern he had explored in painting and drawing since 1958 (Fig. 47). This work, unfortunately, was proofed only twice before the details of drawing were lost, and ten years passed before the artist re-created the composition at the Gemini G.E.L. workshop in Los Angeles. *Alphabets* demonstrates the pitfalls of lithography, particularly when practiced by inexperienced artists and printers. In fact, the printer of *Alphabets* had sufficient knowledge and skill to undertake a more traditional print, but Johns had little notion of the difficulties that would arise in the preparation of a stone that was covered with so many subtle washes of tusche. Johns was less fortunate than Picasso, whose challenge to the most skilled lithographers in France to print his famous *Dove* (also a tusche drawing) is the classic example of the way artists have expanded the possibilities of a medium. One can speculate that had *Alphabets* been among his earliest prints seen by the public, he might have found considerably more encouragement. As it was, *Target, 0 through 9* (a print in which large numbers were superimposed), *Coat Hanger,* and three versions of *Flag* found few purchasers. All these works were printed in black with the exception of two *Flags*—one in white, the other in gray (Fig. 46). Audaciously, one of the *Flags* was printed on tan kraft paper, an affront to the meticulous print connoisseurs of the day.

Figuration was not entirely absent from the art of the 1960s, but where it appeared, it had no relationship to the representative art of the past. Not only was the subject secondary to the process of painting or printing, but it was chosen from entirely new categories, and although parallels could be drawn between Johns's choice of objects and those of Stuart Davis or the nineteenth-century still-life painters, his use of those objects within the compositions was diametrically opposite to his predecessors'.

In the work of Robert Rauschenberg, the representational materials were taken directly from newspaper photos, creating areas of texture in contrast to opulent passages of painterly brushstrokes. Often these photo-mechanically produced images were totally immersed within the heavily brushed passages. Many varieties of inference could be obtained from the subjects of the photos, which aroused emotional responses much as colors do. Rauschenberg's awareness of these subconscious stimuli gave his work a vibrant sense of rhythm: sheep in a meadow and soft couches in a gallery were slow, passive images, while athletes in action were bright, energetic visions. Thus, the figure became only one of several elements in the artist's repertoire rather than the central subject around which the work was composed.

Rauschenberg's background was considerably different from that of Johns or nearly all the younger artists who began printmaking in the 1960s. Fundamentally, Rauschenberg was an experimentalist, formed in the mold of Black Mountain College, where the most audacious creative people found encouragement. There, he met John Cage—the composer whose understanding of process was so exquisite that he could create a work that was pure silence—and attempted to study with Josef Albers, for whom he had little patience. Among Rauschenberg's earliest experiments were a pamphlet of woodcuts all cut from the same block, a series of blueprints of a full-size nude (made by shining a sunlamp on blueprint paper while Susan Weil, Rauschenberg's wife, lay on the sheet), and a twenty-two-foot monoprint of the impression of an automobile tire, made by inking a section of pavement in front of the spread-out paper and driving an automobile over it. These works were made between 1948 and 1951, during and after his first period of study at Black Mountain. He did not return to any form of printmaking until 1962, when he began to silkscreen images onto his canvases and to make lithographs at ULAE. In the intervening decade he had demonstrated the wide range of his interests: he took many fine photographs, designed costumes for modern-dance performances, and created "combine" paintings of found objects, the most newsworthy of which was *Monogram*, a taxidermist's stuffed long-haired goat with an automobile tire around its middle, standing on a painted canvas.

The strange assortment of objects that Rauschenberg brought together in his combines had parallel representatives in his drawings. In 1958 he transferred turpentine-dampened newspaper and magazine illustrations onto paper, their vague outlines enlivened by the energetic and haphazard rubbing marks. These pictures have an unusual, hazy quality, reminiscent of Impressionist paintings, but their nearest relation is Rauschenberg's so-called Dadaist expression, the *Erased de Kooning Drawing* of 1953. In this instance Rauschenberg wanted to see how an eraser could be used "as a drawing tool." Of course, it was important that the drawing he was to erase be recognizable (as were the illustrations he selected from magazines), so that his subsequent action had some foundation in authority, so to speak.

By the time Rauschenberg began to visit ULAE in 1962, bringing with him scraps of illustrations to transfer to stones in the same manner he had used in his drawings, he had established an authentic means of executing two-dimensional works. He elaborated upon Cage's theories of "chance," and was delighted by events that changed the intended outcome of his compositions. The best known of these occurrences happened during the execution of his twelfth print, a large black and white composition created mostly from thickly daubed areas of tusche over the usual "collage" of newspaper illustrations. When the large stone cracked during proofing, Rauschenberg took the small bits of limestone that chipped off and added them to the composition, printed it—huge gaping crack and all—and named it *Accident* (Fig. 50).

Despite Rauschenberg's oft-quoted remark that the twentieth century was no time to begin drawing on rocks, he was the first American to have international success as a lithographer. The popular print competitions that occurred biennially in Yugoslavia, Japan, and Poland offered the possibility of some small renown to the printmakers whose works were recommended by experts from many countries. A print by the American etcher Armin Landeck had won the prize in the first Ljubljana biennial in 1955, but Rauschenberg's victory there in 1963 with *Accident* was more significant, presaging his subsequent triumph in 1964 as the laureate of the Venice Biennale.

Tatyana Grosman encouraged her artists to make books, not in the usual, expected format, of course, but as each artist conceived them as objects within his or her aesthetic. Rauschenberg's penchant for experimenting with the materials of his compositions caused him to pursue both bookmaking and lithography into quite novel areas, and to develop new forms and techniques. While at ULAE in 1964, he created something that he dubbed a "multiple," since there was no term available to categorize an object that was not a print but was produced in an edition, rather like a sculpture but not cast from a mold.★

Shades (Fig. 51) was only nominally a book: a set of five square sheets of Plexiglas held by a metal rack with a sixth sheet, which served as the title page, affixed to the rack behind a light bulb. On each "page" of Rauschenberg's "book" was printed a group of transferred newspaper images held together with the brushstrokes he characteristically used in both prints and paintings at that time. The plates could be put into the metal frame in different sequences, and each could be inserted in any of eight directions, involving the viewer much as the Happenings did.

Rauschenberg made *Shades* and several large-scale lithographs at the time that he became active in dance as a performer and in experimental activities with Billy Kluver, the engineer with whom he later founded E.A.T. (Experiments in Art and Technology). The purpose of E.A.T. was to bring artists and engineers together to evolve works of art which would grow out of the interchange between the creative imagination and technological expertise. The first manifestation of this idea, which actually predated the formal founding of E.A.T. in 1966, was a performance at the same Armory where the famous American debut of modern art had taken place in 1913. It was an expensive but disappointing public event that left Rauschenberg in dire financial straits. He was unable to resist the lure of a contract offered by Ken Tyler, a former Tamarind master printer who had set up his new lithographic Gemini G.E.L. workshop in Los Angeles specifically to attract artists who already had well-established reputations.

Prints made by the emerging painters whose work was characterized as Pop Art—the artists for whom Johns and Rauschenberg represented a sort of stepping-stone—

★The concept of the multiple appears to have been invented in 1959 by a group of European artists who produced such works under the name of MAT (Multiplication of Transformable Art). Some of them were members of the loosely organized, Neo-Dadaist Fluxus group. Like the Dadaists of 1916, who had taken to the cabarets of Zurich to project their nihilistic message through outrageous words, actions, and appearance, they staged performances, events that became known in the late 1950s as Happenings. They often used as props objects they had made themselves, which were occasionally preserved as artworks. These objects, made outside the boundaries of traditional studio or workshop art, were a catalyst for three-dimensional work being done within the print workshop.

form the core of the explosion into public awareness of the print in the 1960s. Two of the so-called Pop Artists (a term that has been subjected to considerable and frequent modification as each artist has averred that it did not describe either his work or his motivation) began their careers with the notoriety conferred by their Happenings. Claes Oldenburg and Jim Dine created some of the most memorable Happenings, influenced by Allan Kaprow, the pioneer of this art form, whose ideas led directly into Conceptual and Performance Art. But however much they developed their Happenings as preordained events mirroring daily life in its most extreme actions and reactions, both Dine and Oldenburg were concerned with the visual element more than the dramatic or intellectual.

Oldenburg was six years older than Dine, but the two artists had one talent in common, the ability to draw extremely well. They each made a few early prints at the Pratt Graphic Art Center, which was just around the corner from their studios. Oldenburg's included quickly sketched lithographs of a pie and *Table Top with Objects*, executed in 1961 (the year in which he opened The Store, the site of ten Happenings), the etching *Orpheum Sign,* and another etching, of legs, also done in 1961.

Oldenburg's most memorable and significant "print" of the 1960s was, in reality, a multiple, his *Tea Bag* (Fig. 53). This work was a result of the widening awareness that brought new people into the business of art. Recognizing that the multiple filled a gap in the market, Barbara Kulicke, Marion Goodman, Robert Graham, Ursula Kalish, and Sonny Sloan founded a combination gallery–publishing house named Multiples in 1965, with an inventory consisting of the 1964 output of MAT. Multiples's first publication was *Four on Plexiglas* (published in 1966), works by Philip Guston, Barnett Newman, Larry Rivers—and Oldenburg's *Tea Bag,* a silkscreen on vacuum-formed Plexiglas, the contours of which followed a printed piece of felt that looked like a giant tea bag.

Oldenburg was essentially a sculptor, so it was logical that he would choose Plexiglas as a forming medium, even though the works in *Four on Plexiglas* were meant to be hung on a wall. Throughout the 1960s he preferred objects to prints when he worked within the publishing establishment. Among his multiples of the period were *London Knees* (published by Editions Alecto in London with postcards and other reproductions of drawings in 1968) and the majestic swimming-pool-blue, polyurethane-over-lithograph *Profile Airflow* (published by Gemini G.E.L. in 1969). He created a set of lithographs at Gemini, *Notes* (1968), that emulated his sketchbook drawings, but he did not devote serious time to printmaking on paper until the 1970s.

Jim Dine, on the other hand, not only made twenty or so drypoints at Pratt at the time he executed his prints for *The International Avant Garde,* but he also drew six lithographs there in 1960 that referred to his Happening, *Car Crash.* Like many art students of the 1950s, he had made several woodcuts, and seemed to have a natural way with printmaking. In 1962 he was invited to ULAE. He spent parts of each year from 1962 to 1965 there, working on lithographs that extended the shop's expertise (one print, *Cut and Snip,* was appropriately made on two sheets of paper; another, *White Teeth,* was printed in white on black paper). Dine tended to work in series: there were four prints titled *Toothbrush,* two versions of *Bathroom* (*Black* and *Pink*), and four compositions based on a traditional artist's palette. Common objects, such as men's ties and bathrobes, toothbrushes and carpenter's tools, were affixed to Dine's canvases and represented in his prints. He removed the human element (still present in Johns's work and in the highly selective nature of Rauschenberg's choice of objects) from the work of art as much as possible. Nevertheless, Dine's vision was never impersonal; his use of a bathrobe and painter's palette certainly indicates that the artist himself was his own subject.

It was Dine's removal of the object from human context that characterized his work as Pop. The objects are not positioned either carefully or casually by the artist, as in traditional still life; they are simply transposed from their usual environment to an artistic one where their value or function is solely relational. In the 1962 lithograph *Four C Clamps* (Fig. 54), Dine lines up these devices across the top of the composition as he had hung up a variety of real tools in his "combine" painting *Five Feet of Colorful Tools* (1962), forming a sort of frieze. The drips from the brushed drawing of the clamps in the lithographs are reminders about art and illusion. They serve to emphasize the rough-surfaced handmade paper, so that there is no doubt that this is only a lithograph, not a picture of reality. This simple print is one of the first in which the use of special paper (a rustic, yellow-toned French paper made in one of Europe's oldest mills) is a particular feature of the work, a harbinger of the next decade's increasing interest in paper textures and colors, as well as in the manufacture of paper both for prints and as material for multiple art in and of itself.

Dine's work with Tatyana Grosman came to a temporary halt in 1965. The following year he moved to London, where he worked on several projects including an album of silkscreens with photographs and other collage elements—*Tool Box,* printed by the innovative Chris Prater—and etchings based on Oscar Wilde's *The Picture of Dorian Gray.* He met the Pop Artists of England: Edouardo Paolozzi, the transplanted American R. B. Kitaj, and Richard Hamilton, whose 1957 definition of Pop more or less covered the intentions of most of the artists on both sides of the Atlantic:

> Popular (designed for a mass audience), transient (short-term solution), expendable (easily forgotten), low cost, mass-produced, young (aimed at youth), witty, sexy, gimmicky, glamourous, big business.*

James Rosenquist was the second Pop Artist to work at ULAE. He had earned money during his student days in Minnesota and later in New York by painting the very large and colorful billboards that are such a characteristic element in the American landscape. He found in the partly new, partly old signs a stroboscopic view that paralleled the adjustments the human eye makes when it considers its surroundings. The same understanding of the multiplicity of the stimuli from which the mind selects what it will pay attention to is seen in the art of Robert Rauschenberg, but Rauschenberg softens the discontinuity of the objects with brushstrokes that draw the disparate elements together. Rosenquist was younger than Rauschenberg, and without ties to action painting. When he presented the images that he "found" in the context of partially obliterated billboards, he reveled in their patchy inconsistency, not in the remnants of activity that were revealed.

As Rosenquist began to make lithographs, he had to face the challenge of translating his interest in commercially designed material into print without losing sight of the nearly photographic representations that were his inspiration. His solution was to use airbrush and stencil, which in his second lithograph, *Campaign* (1965), gave a softness to his rendering of a set of army campaign ribbons, a box of Kleenex, and a saltshaker, surrounded by stenciled bedroom wallpaper. *Spaghetti and Grass* (Fig. 57), also made at ULAE in this period, is, in its way, a much more abstract

---

*In a letter to Alison and Peter Smithson, January 16, 1957. Quoted in *Richard Hamilton,* intro. by Richard Morphet (London: Tate Gallery, 1970). It is difficult, in discussing this period, to divorce American art entirely from certain elements in British art. David Hockney, for example, made several of his earliest prints in the 1960s at Pratt, and then went to Los Angeles, where he preceded Albers and Rauschenberg at Gemini G.E.L. The portfolio he created there was published by Editions Alecto as *A Hollywood Collection;* Alecto also published Dine's *Tool Box.* Paul Cornwall-Jones, a director of Alecto, later founded Petersburg Press, where he published *The Picture of Dorian Gray* and many other prints by Dine, Johns, and other Americans in the 1970s and '80s.

work. Divided into two parts, with stylized advertising-art grass at the bottom and mammoth, writhing "Franco-American"–type spaghetti at the top, it is Pop Art's evocation of a typical Rothko composition and an early example of the tendency to quote earlier artists and earlier styles within the constructs of Pop.

Rosenquist continued to make a few prints each year, some at ULAE, others for the dealer Richard Feigen, who opened a gallery just for prints and multiples in Bonwit Teller's Fifth Avenue department store in 1968. In the 1970s Rosenquist also worked at Hollander Workshop and the University of South Florida. After he completed his four-panel mural paintings *F-111* (1965) and *Horse Blinders* (1968–69), and other monumental horizontal works, Rosenquist tended to compose his prints in that format. He made print versions of *Horse Blinders* in 1972 for Multiples and *F-111* in 1974 for Petersburg Press. At first silkscreen and lithography were combined by the printers at Styria Studio and at Petersburg for the large prints, but in his single-panel *Off the Continental Divide,* printed at ULAE in 1975–76, Rosenquist was able to use the offset lithography proofing press. Subsequently, Rosenquist made many lithographs and etchings that convey the plastic, spastic energy of contemporary life. Through his choice of objects, patterns, and conjunctions, he has transformed this impulse into panoramas of our visually aggressive environment.

The portfolio *Ten Works by Ten Painters,* issued in 1964 by the Wadsworth Atheneum of Hartford, Connecticut, under the direction of its curator of painting, Samuel Wagstaff, Jr., contained silkscreens after compositions made specially by the artists (and, thus, was for too long considered "not original"). It was the first set of prints (aside from the illustrations in *1¢ Life*) to include some typical works of the Pop Artists. In a quirky but prescient selection, the images of Stuart Davis, Robert Indiana, Ellsworth Kelly, Roy Lichtenstein, Robert Motherwell, George Ortman, Larry Poons, Ad Reinhardt, Frank Stella, and Andy Warhol were put side by side. The Wadsworth portfolio, concentrating as it did on silkscreen (it was produced in Connecticut by Ives-Sillman), was a cohesive work because the imagery of each artist, with the possible exception of Motherwell, depended upon flat color and sharp edges.

New York 10, published by Rosa Esman's Tanglewood Press in 1965 (the year of the "print explosion"), was the second portfolio to showcase the new artists. In the late 1950s Mrs. Esman had opened the small Tanglewood Gallery in Rockwell Kent's old studio in Stockbridge, Massachusetts, where she and her psychiatrist husband had a summer home. The gallery specialized in contemporary American work, showing small paintings by newer artists like Indiana and Wesselmann alongside woodcuts by Milton Avery. In the winter Mrs. Esman sold prints to architects in

New York City for the adornment of the offices they designed. Her idea of publishing her own prints was encouraged by another psychiatrist, her friend Hans Kleinschmidt, whose interest in Dada, updated by the ephemeral publications of the European and American avant-garde which he collected, inspired in him the desire to make art accessible to many at low cost. With his help and that of Doris Freedman, Tanglewood Press was founded and soon published, at $100 an album, *New York 10* and *New York International.* Pop was represented in *New York 10* by Dine, Nicholas Krushenick, Lichtenstein, Oldenburg (his first color lithograph, made with Irwin Hollander), George Segal, and Tom Wesselmann; also included were works by Richard Anuszkiewicz, Helen Frankenthaler, Robert Kulicke, and Mon Levinson, friends of the publisher with few stylistic affinities with one another or with the Pop Artists.

The most ambitious of Rosa Esman's projects, *11 Pop Artists,* issued in 1965, was a set of three portfolios, each a different size. Each portfolio contained a work by Allan d'Arcangelo, Jim Dine (Fig. 55), Allen Jones, Gerald Laing, Roy Lichtenstein (Fig. 59), Peter Philips, Mel Ramos, James Rosenquist, Andy Warhol (Fig. 61), John Wesley, and Tom Wesselmann. *11 Pop Artists,* which included some of Lichtenstein's most important prints, melded together the Pop Artists of England and America. All of the prints were silkscreens, the preferred medium of these artists, whose works derived, at least in formal terms, from commercially manufactured materials. At last the legacy of the WPA and FAP silkscreen workshops of the 1930s had found its most appropriate form. Also contributing to the importance of *11 Pop Artists* was its sponsorship by Philip Morris, which circulated the prints in Europe and thereby broadened public interest in the Pop movement.

The last project to involve the Pop Artists that Esman produced was *Ten for Castelli* (1967), objects and prints by the artists of his gallery from Bontecou to Warhol. For the first time Esman was able to work with Jasper Johns, who insisted on creating a work that was as different as possible from the prints he had made at ULAE, for he felt that doing otherwise would be disloyal to Tatyana Grosman. Yet another Esman project was KMF, an organization she founded to produce both prints and multiples. In 1965 KMF issued *7 in a Box,* which included Oldenburg's multiple *Baked Potato.*

Ten Works by Ten Painters and *New York 10* were notable for many reasons, including the fact that they presented single prints by Roy Lichtenstein in the context of what the other Pop Artists were doing. Considerably more experienced than the others,

Lichtenstein immediately seemed to have a sense of authority when he turned to the comic strip and its compositional details as the subject of his painting. He insisted that his choice was made on formal rather than subjective grounds, and indeed his compositions are presented as flat patterns of unmodulated lines, dots (taken from the Ben Day dot pattern that created tone in the cheaply reproduced comic-strip drawings), and isolated plain forms. Lichtenstein's first prints, with compositions already derived from offset printing, were produced on an offset press in 1964 for the Castelli Gallery. They were not taken seriously as original prints, as they had exactly the same subjects as his paintings (although unrelated to them formally). His silkscreen prints for *Ten Works by Ten Painters* and *New York 10* were on plastic and, again, were ambiguous as fine-art prints. Finally, in *11 Pop Artists,* Lichtenstein's prints joined those of other artists and were accepted as original imagery. *Sweet Dreams, Baby! (POW)* and *Reverie* were much more colorful than the paintings that preceded them, owing probably to the saturation of the silkscreen paints that were used.

Lichtenstein's use of familiar images as a starting point for his compositions dominated his work in print, first in the *Brushstrokes* he made with Irwin Hollander in 1966 (a witty commentary upon action painting); then in the lithographs he made with Ken Tyler at Gemini in 1969, based on Monet's two series of atmospheric paintings of Rheims cathedral (Fig. 60) and of haystacks; and finally in a sequence of progressively abstract bulls, loosely derived from Theo van Doesburg's works on the same theme. In these later works, Lichtenstein's tenuous Pop Artist identification is clearly abandoned. He had long been fascinated by the compositions and stylistic idiosyncrasies of other, earlier modern artists. In these Gemini prints he dwelt particularly upon the serial nature of some of these works from the past. His attention to the types of emphasis that created "style" led him to present elements of Art Deco, or Art Moderne, in the context of his own formula. Lichtenstein's appropriation of what was then considered an unimpressive decorative style, and his penchant for multiple new views of subjects used by artists of the past, were both influential factors in the development of other artists' styles at the end of the 1960s.

Repetition of the image, however, was not Lichtenstein's exclusive domain. Print, which made pure repetition a simple mechanical process, was the essential medium of Pop Art's most succinct representative, Andy Warhol. He too "discovered" the comic strip; when he found that Lichtenstein had long ago appropriated it, it did not take him long to find another source of imagery, one that would fulfill his desire to distinguish his work from others' and literally be a "hit." Having started his New York career as a successful commercial artist, Warhol was more than familiar with graphics and was quick to see the special qualities of printed material that could be exploited by transposition to larger scale, emphasis of detail, repetition, and addition of color. His choices of subject were particularly important since they had to be familiar in several ways: daily use or awareness of a product (such as Campbell's Soup or Brillo); public personality, usually overexposed and thereby already abstracted in form by the news mediums (such as Marilyn Monroe or Jackie Kennedy); and disasters, again rendered abstract by the uniformity imposed by the mediums. Once his choices had been made, Warhol turned to stencil to add his personal detail to the subjects, using unmodulated, flat, and nearly lifeless paint to create large canvases, repeating in checkerboard fashion, over and over again, the familiar image. Consciously confronting the revered American concept of "originality," he used print as a means of declaring independence from old rules and habits.

His "paintings" and prints on paper were produced in similar ways: the young artists who worked in his "Factory" would follow his instructions as to which screen to use in what format, the screens having been made commercially from enlarged photographs chosen by Warhol. Unlike Rauschenberg, who silkscreened images from newspapers and magazines onto canvases only to mask them with brushstrokes and applied objects, Warhol seemed intent on repudiating the artist's presence in the work of art. He limited himself to deciding how the news photo, reduced to a pattern of dots, would be enlarged, what other screens would be added in order to emphasize certain features of the photograph, and what colors would be used for these and additional screens.

Warhol used the same silkscreens for both unlimited and limited editions of prints on paper and for his canvases. Although they are not included in the catalogue of his original prints, his first extensive print project was a set of screens depicting four flowers (Fig. 62). Thousands of the same unsigned image were printed. Although he contributed a print to *Ten Works by Ten Painters* in 1964, it was not until he made three prints with news photos of Jackie Kennedy for *11 Pop Artists* (Fig. 61) that he began to limit the editions of his silkscreens. Printed solely in black on metallic backgrounds, the three Jackie prints represent the "still" version of Warhol's film-making style, in which he repeated one or a limited number of movements over and over. The newspaper images of the mourning First Lady are "flashes" of a real event without its substance.

Warhol often used the same photographic image, with color variations, in a series of individual prints. The first album of this sort was *Ten Marilyns* (1967). The colors are the fluorescent, acid hues that shout out from cheap advertising signs. Their use as a means of emphasizing the false façade of the tragic actress, or, in his *Flowers* prints, the deadness of the omnipresent fake flowers of modern life, show Warhol to be more of a social commentator than was then apparent. (He also made albums of his Campbell's Soup labels.) But it was not until later in the 1970s that changes in his compositional style injected some sense of personality into his prints.

Warhol's career in the 1960s was as nearly that of the Renaissance man as he could make it. He lived his art, not only as a creator of images and director of studios, but as a personality, like those Hollywood stars who transform themselves into the movie characters that their fans believe them actually to be. In the twentieth-century art world the most famous transformation of this kind was that of Salvador Dali; Warhol's "artist" owes much to his example and the Dadaist seed from which it grew. As with Dali, Warhol's public persona made awareness of his art much more widespread. This was also enhanced by his production of prints, since their multiplicity gave the public a degree of familiarity with the style of the artist beyond that obtainable through museum and gallery exhibitions of unique pieces.

The audacity of Warhol's imagery had considerable impact, but other artists with parallel interests in commercialized visual information also contributed to the Pop movement. Robert Indiana, who "starred" in Warhol's movie *Eat,* concentrated upon the power of signboard lettering to transmute words into abstract designs and thus induce Pavlovian responses to artistic form. Inspired by product labels and stylized renderings of photographs or symbols, Indiana illuminated the graphic designer's idiosyncrasies in his paintings and prints and with pure, bright color and sharp definition dashed them off as art. Like Warhol and Lichtenstein, Indiana often made serial prints. His first portfolio, *Numbers,* with text by Robert Creeley, was published and screenprinted in Europe by Domberger in 1968.

One of Indiana's images, a logo-inspired rendering of the word "love" in red, white, blue, and green, was such a popular success that it became the hula hoop of art. *LOVE* was made by Indiana first as a painting, then an unlimited edition of silkscreens, then a three-dimensional metal multiple, then limited-edition prints in several forms and colors (Fig. 63), and finally, having become universally familiar, it was "ripped off" by sophisticated merchandisers and hippies alike to become the most pervasive emblem of the "flower power" generation. Among its later, authorized manifestations was an American postage stamp.

Tom Wesselmann had taken the familiar academic image of the female nude and painted her among the dime-store decorations of the "typical" American home. In his prints of the 1960s, Wesselmann presented the nude and her surroundings of radios, refrigerators, and plastic fruit in flatly rendered forms with standardized paintbox colors that silkscreen made even more suggestive of impersonal existence (Fig. 64). For *New York 10* he made an inkless intaglio print (a form of embossing that Albers had introduced into fine-art printing in America in the 1950s, although it had been popularized in the 1890s and continued to be used as a form of candy-box decoration). The print depicted a cheap Bakelite radio, one of the still-life elements that usually accompanied Wesselmann's nudes. He also made vacuum-formed plastic and watercolored inkless prints of nudes. The single breast he presented in a print included in a portfolio issued in Germany in 1968 titled *Graphik USA* (which also included Indiana's *German LOVE* in the national colors) was immediately identifiable as Wesselmann's, a fundamental requisite for Pop Art imagery.

The two sculptors active in the 1960s whose work seemed most akin to the Pop spirit were Marisol and George Segal. Later the works of both were seen to have come from influences quite unlike those that motivated the Pop Artists discussed above, but their brashness and dependence upon the crass and familiar categorized them as Pop at the time of their appearance. Marisol, a Venezuelan who grew up in Paris, made figures from raw wood, then painted or drew realistic facial features directly upon the wood and added molded hands and feet where appropriate. Her prints and multiples dwelled upon hands, feet, and faces (she rarely detailed anything in between). Her subjects in sculpture were often "high-profile" personalities, such as presidents and movie stars, so that when she made a few prints with only details of what was presented in her sculpture, their peculiar use of color and shape was easily identified as hers (Fig. 66). Her drawing style, mainly crayon strokes with colors apparently chosen at random from a Crayola box, was the same manner she used in the lithographs she made at ULAE in 1965. She later made several etchings at ULAE and an extraordinarily large, two-sheet lithographic self-portrait made from an impression of her own nude body.

George Segal's life-size figures of white plaster were placed within settings of real furniture and architectural elements taken, without transformation, from their functional environment. Segal also drew from the figure, mainly in pastel, and his few early prints attempted to present his cropped figures in the context of chalky silkscreens. A much more successful, and far more suitable, set of prints of varying scale were made in 1975 on very large etching plates in Rome. Segal had several people in blue jeans transfer their bodily imprints onto the sensitized plates (Fig. 68). These huge, darkly moody prints, made with human beings in just as active a role as when he made his plaster figures by wrapping his subjects in plaster-wet rags, have an expressive quality that reveals that Segal did not have the cool, offhand temperament of the Pop Artist.

The story of Pop Art and its impact upon the craft of printmaking is incomplete without the inclusion of artists who worked elsewhere than in New York: its early adherents in England, and the Californians who presented a more romantically assimilated view of plastic culture. As has been noted, about half of the artists whose works were included in *11 Pop Artists* were British. Although Richard Hamilton, who more or less founded the Pop movement, was *not* included, one of his most compelling images, *Solomon R. Guggenheim Museum*, was a contemporaneous example of a print that bridged the two wings of the movement (the image was taken from a postcard sent to Hamilton by the then curator of the museum, the British art historian and first critic of Pop Art, Lawrence K. Alloway). Only in the 1970s did Hamilton actually make prints in America, but his physical presence here was not necessary for his ideas to have a profound influence. Similarly, the works of the expatriate R. B. Kitaj, who lived in England and made his collage-type silkscreens only there, were exhibited at the New York branch of Marlborough Gallery and thus were as visible as those of any local artist. Kitaj's was a synoptic view of culture, somewhat more intellectual than Pop Art was supposed to be (Fig. 56). Allen Jones, whose sexually exaggerated females represented a British view of Pop culture, made three sets of prints at Tamarind in 1966.

None of the foremost New York Pop Artists worked at Tamarind, but the British liked to go out to Southern California and mingle with local Pop practitioners such as Ed Ruscha and H. C. Westermann. The latter made a set of prints at Tamarind that reflected the same zany view of the material world that he incorporated into his proto-Pop constructions. His portfolio, *See America First* (1968, Fig. 70), was a deluxe, running caricature on Western (meaning Far West) culture. With other Western artists like William T. Crutchfield and William T. Wiley, Westermann produced his own fanciful world which begged his relationship to Pop and made clear that when the entire environment was already Pop itself, its use as subject matter made little impact.

Only Ruscha made silkscreen prints that abstracted the familiar Southern California forms into cool, aggressively Pop compositions. His large *Standard Station* of 1966 (Fig. 71) and his silkscreens of the large sign that looms above Hollywood and labels it were the kind of prints that successfully passed on the Pop message. His paintings and prints of single words, executed in trompe-l'oeil style, as if they had been spit out or written in an appropriate liquid, were his stylistic signatures, characteristic and provocative affronts to good taste. The many lithographs he made at Tamarind in 1969 are only rarely more than sketches of his subjects, except when they are printed in color. The garish rainbow or ombre-effect that he preferred in his backgrounds became a cliché of fine printmaking in the late 1960s.

Lithography did not seem to be a suitable means of translating the most pungent Pop messages into print; although Nicholas Krushenick, working at Tamarind, was able to extract from the medium the purest, most saturated inkings, most of his prints took on a soft, arty quality that was the opposite of the slick appearance characteristic of the movement (Fig. 65). When Lichtenstein went to Los Angeles to make prints at Gemini in 1969, he often combined lithography with embossing or silkscreen. Although it had previously been considered contaminating and inefficient to have two different print processes within the same studio (and the mediums are still kept well separated, for practical reasons), the "print explosion" generated a need for facilities that could provide artists with professional printers, suitable materials, and, ultimately, convenience. Many small enterprises were founded which did research into the ancient secrets of papermaking and ink manufacture, and a frenetic search for skills ensued. The new forms required many specialized techniques which were to be found within the commercial establishment; this led to what was elegantly dubbed "the yellow pages aesthetic."

By the late 1960s, many artists whose imagery was less enmeshed in predigested graphic formulae than that of the Pop Artists had begun to make prints, and there was a general acknowledgment that nearly any painter worthy of being considered important would have to make prints as well. This was the period when the vision of a creative society proclaimed by John F. Kennedy was subjected to the radical re-evaluation that led to race riots, assassinations, student upheavals, drug use, and a war that no one understood. The pulling apart of the American spirit had its parallel in the many forms of expression flourishing in the visual arts. No diminution of the economy occurred to produce abrupt disruptions of the art market, and the publication of prints went on in full force, now responsive to many more artistic interests. Foremost among these interests was an examination of the properties inherent in the art object, not only its physical structure but its relationship to the environment into which it was introduced and to the society that beheld it. Nearly every manifestation of this examination (as well as the continuing styles of the previous decades) was expressed in some form of print, and some depended upon prints entirely.

36. Willem de Kooning. Untitled. 1960. Lithograph, 42¾ x 30¾″ (108.6 x 78.0 cm.). The Museum of Modern Art, New York, gift of Mrs. Bliss Parkinson

The bravura of de Kooning's first lithograph derives, in part, from the notable absence of intention to perform technical acrobatics in the formation of the composition. There is no better word in the vocabulary of art than "spontaneity" when the mind and hand of the artist together exercise his intelligence, the control learned from years of practice, physical power, and the creative depth to achieve it. The audacity of this composition, familiar in texture, perhaps, to the aficionado of Oriental calligraphy, has an overwhelmingly exciting impression that no calligraphic sign can provide. The spatters of ink rush to escape looming masses of brushstrokes, while clustered sprinkles representing the liquid basis of lithography invade the more massive forms. Punctured by their dissolving action, the heavier areas of ink acquire even more energy. Printed on poor paper (fine rag paper was still unavailable in the size needed for such a large print), there is no pretentiousness in de Kooning's debut in the medium.

The appearance of a print by such a famous artist, at a moment when his drawings and paintings had a wide and appreciative audience, had no precedent. From an economic point of view (a subject of considerable importance for prints, which unlike unique works are commodities in a broad market), de Kooning's lithographs presented an astonishing situation: within two years they were selling at the same level as Picasso's colorful linoleum cuts, while the works of even the most important or best-known American printmakers still commanded only half their price. De Kooning's prints, therefore, may be seen as forecasting the burgeoning impact on the art market of works by American painters in the print mediums.

37. Willem de Kooning. *Woman in Amagansett*. 1970. Published by
M. Knoedler & Co., Inc., New York. Lithograph, 23¹⁄₁₆ x 31″
(58.5 x 78.8 cm.)

38. Robert Motherwell. *In Black with Yellow Ochre*. 1963. Published
by Universal Limited Art Editions. Lithograph, 18⅛ x 13⅞″
(46.0 x 35.2 cm.). Courtesy Stanley and Renie Helfgott

39. Barnett Newman. *Cantos VII, VIII,* and *IX* from *18 Cantos.* 1963–64. Published by Universal Limited Art Editions. Lithographs, 14¾ x 13⅛" (37.5 x 33.3 cm.)

"These cantos arose from a compelling necessity—the result of grappling with the instrument. To me that is what lithography is. It is an instrument." In his introduction to *18 Cantos,* Barnett Newman examines his relationship as an artist to lithography and how he "plays" it. His use of the metaphor "instrument" to relate lithography to music—eventually he characterizes the *Cantos* as a "symphonic mass . . . each canto adds its song to the full chorus"—indicates clearly why he created this extended set of prints and how they were achieved.

From the outset, Newman realized that his composition would consist not only of what he drew on the lithographic stone, but also of the areas of paper surrounding the printed mass. As he developed each composition, often using the same stones but printing in different colors or sequence, he would have proofs made on a variety of papers. Each margin

had to have unique proportion in relation to the printed area, sometimes meeting the edge of the ink, sometimes forming a wide and airy border. The color and texture of the paper itself altered the surface of the printed area.

As the eye moves from print to print, one gets the impression of an uninterrupted rhythm quite unlike that obtained from seeing a row of paintings in different lights. It is a private experience in which nearly identical imagery expands and contracts, vibrates with intense color or soothes with the identical palette, and impels the viewer to continue the journey on to the next and the next. When Newman began the series, he planned to execute only three prints (the number he had made at Pratt in 1961), but the potential of the medium compelled him to continue, from seven to fourteen to eighteen. While he admitted that each print was a separate entity (and they are formally housed in a portfolio that allows them to be viewed only one at a time), he felt that for each *Canto* the "fullest meaning . . . is when it is seen together with the others."

40. OPPOSITE ABOVE Sam Francis. *The Upper Yellow.* 1960. Published by Klipstein and Kornfeld, Berne. Lithograph, 24⅞ x 35¹¹⁄₁₆″ (63.2 x 90.6 cm.). The Museum of Modern Art, New York, D. S. and R. H. Gottesman Foundation Fund

41. OPPOSITE BELOW Adolph Gottlieb. *Germination II.* 1969. Published by Marlborough Graphics, New York. Lithograph, 22¼ x 30″ (56.5 x 76.2 cm.). Courtesy Marlborough Gallery, New York

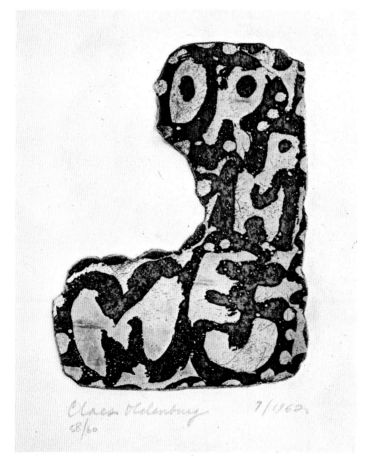

42. Claes Oldenburg. *Orpheum Sign* from *The International Avant Garde,* Vol. 5, *America Discovered.* 1962. Published by Gallerie Schwarz, Milan. Etching and aquatint, 5⅞ x 4⁷⁄₁₆″ (14.9 x 11.3 cm.). The Museum of Modern Art, New York, gift of Peter Deitsch Gallery

43. Andy Warhol. *Cooking Pot* from *The International Avant Garde,* Vol. 5, *America Discovered.* 1962. Published by Gallerie Schwarz, Milan. Photo-engraving, 6³⁄₁₆ x 4⅝″ (15.7 x 11.7 cm.). The Museum of Modern Art, New York, gift of Peter Deitsch Gallery

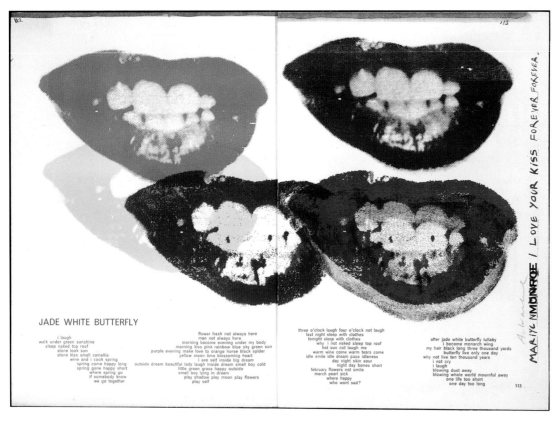

44. Andy Warhol. *Marilyn Monroe I Love Your Kiss Forever Forever* from *1¢ Life* by Walasse Ting. 1964. Published by E. W. Kornfeld, Paris. Lithograph, 11⅝ x 21¼″ (29.5 x 54.0 cm.)

45. Roy Lichtenstein. *Fresh Air 1$25¢* from *1¢ Life* by Walasse Ting. 1964. Published by E. W. Kornfeld, Paris. Lithograph, 12¾ x 22″ (32.5 x 55.9 cm.)

46. Jasper Johns. *Flag III*. 1960. Published by Universal Limited Art Editions. Lithograph, 17½ x 26¾″ (44.5 x 67.9 cm.). Brooke Alexander, Inc.

47. ABOVE Jasper Johns. *Alphabets*. 1962. Lithograph, 34¼ x 23¹¹⁄₁₆″ (87.0 x 60.2 cm.). The Museum of Modern Art, New York, acquired with matching funds from James K. Epstein and the National Endowment for the Arts

48. OPPOSITE Jasper Johns. *Hatteras*. 1963. Published by Universal Limited Art Editions. Lithograph, 38¼ x 29⅛″ (97.2 x 74.0 cm.)

In the 1960s Jasper Johns often lived in Edisto Beach, South Carolina, down the Atlantic coast from Cape Hatteras, the famous site of storms off North Carolina. The name alone induces predictable responses, so firmly is it associated with the hurricane season. As a geographical entity it is a rather dangerous place to be, a place to look out for danger, and a signal. It represents several concepts at once: caution, indication, and signification. Presenting a composition titled *Hatteras*, Johns offers data that allude to those ideas: an imprint of an arm that seems to have signaled to one side, thus creating a symbol or sign in the form of a circle; three bands labeled with the names of colors, although the bands themselves are not colored and it is not at all certain that the words indicate

the colors correctly, even though we are prepared to accept their visual information; a vague shape that disconcertingly intrudes onto the circle (from other works by Johns of this time it may be identified as the imprint of a foot on sand) which Johns has circled, perhaps cautioning that it needs to be excised.

Hatteras is a print made during a period in which Johns inserted many doubts or paradoxical references into his work. It was his largest print up to that time and one of the first that was partly invented within the medium (the painting *Periscope* [*Hart Crane*], named from a quote in Crane's poem "Cape Hatteras," is similar in composition but lacks the breadth of circular gesture and the imprint of the foot). The broad sweep of the arm's circular path in *Hatteras* brings to mind the classic Renaissance image, Alberti's diagram of a man within a circle, which shows the measure of ideal human proportion. The reversed scale of numbers at the bottom of Johns's print, another indicator of measurement, confronts the viewer once again with the ambiguity of the relation between signs and their significance. No matter what intellectual exercise may be derived from Johns's work, there is abundant satisfaction for one who only looks and feels.

49. ABOVE Jasper Johns. *Decoy*. 1971. Published by Universal Limited Art Editions. Offset lithograph, 41 x 29″ (104.1 x 73.7 cm.). Courtesy of Wolfgang Wittrock

In 1966–67 Johns created several prints using photographed elements from his paintings and bronze sculptures. These works (*Passage I* and *II*, *Watchman*, *Voice*, and *First Etchings*) incorporated ghostlike photographic images of limbs, sliding panels, forks and spoons, and his sculptural renditions of objects (light bulb, flashlight, coffee can containing paintbrushes, and the open and unopened Ballantine Ale cans that, in their purely drawn lithographic version of 1964, became Johns's most famous print). In 1967, after completing *Watchman*, Johns began an even larger lithograph, which was to

become *Decoy* four years later. In the interim Johns concentrated upon making etchings at ULAE's new etching studio and several series of lithographs at Gemini G.E.L. in California. When he returned to his unfinished lithograph, ULAE had acquired an offset proofing press which Tatyana Grosman intended to use for the production of catalogues of her prints. The idea of making images directly upon plates that would not be reversed in the printing process, and obtaining proofs at a much faster rate (consequently allowing a more natural, connected creative concentration), inspired Johns. *Decoy* is crowded with images that nudge at memories of previous works: bent letters spelling out primary and secondary colors (only the "violet" may be read entirely), and the famous ale

can, by now a sort of icon of contemporary art, sitting in the middle. The lower portion, devoted to the bronze sculptures, recollects the friezes of small boxes atop two of Johns's early target paintings, which contained casts of human body parts. Finally, there is the thin line that overlays this passage, a rainbow or color spectrum (Johns had first used the rainbow "roll" in his lithograph *Pinion* in 1963) illuminating another photographed element that is interrupted in the middle by a hole cut through the paper. Johns had told Tatyana Grosman that the hole was meant to be a way to "escape," so that it seems that *Decoy*, like *Watchman*, was viewed by the artist as a means of trapping the viewer, one of the painter's most fundamental aims.

50. Robert Rauschenberg. *Accident*. 1963. Published by Universal Limited Art Editions. Lithograph, 38½ x 27¼" (97.8 x 69.0 cm.)

51. ABOVE Robert Rauschenberg. *Shades.* 1964. Published by Universal Limited Art Editions. Lithographs on six Plexiglas panels, frame 15 x 14 x 12″ (38.1 x 35.5 x 30.5 cm.). Brooke Alexander, Inc.

52. OPPOSITE Robert Rauschenberg. *Booster.* 1967. Published by Gemini G.E.L. Lithograph and silkscreen, 71⁹⁄₁₆ x 35⅛″ (181.8 x 89.2 cm.). © copyright Gemini G.E.L., Los Angeles, California, 1967

When Rauschenberg decided to leave Tatyana Grosman and work with Ken Tyler in Los Angeles, it was a decided disturbance in the family feeling at ULAE. But the group of eight prints he made during his first project at Gemini allowed him to experiment with some freedom, working up ideas for the very large print Tyler had in mind when he asked Rauschenberg to work with him. The nearly six-foot-high image that was devised from some elements in the seven study prints has as its central focus a five-part X-ray of the artist. Like his

three-panel billboard print, *Autobiography* (photo-offset on three five-and-one-half by four-foot sheets in 1968), *Booster* is a self-portrait, utilizing not only the artist's image (stripped to the bones, to be sure), but also a chair which was incorporated in several works of the period as a very personal object, first as a prop in a dance by Steve Paxton and again in Rauschenberg's unique works silkscreened on Plexiglas: *Revolver* (1967), *Solstice,* and *Soundings* (1968). A time chart for 1967 is silkscreened in red over the lower part of the composition. Given Rauschenberg's interest in the space program (he had made a collage dedicated to the first man to walk in space in 1965), there is no question that the title, *Booster,* refers to one of the stages of a rocket. Besides the jump in scale that this print represents, its other claim to innovation is the combination of silkscreen and lithography, which became increasingly common as artists became more involved in printmaking and understood better the characteristics of each medium.

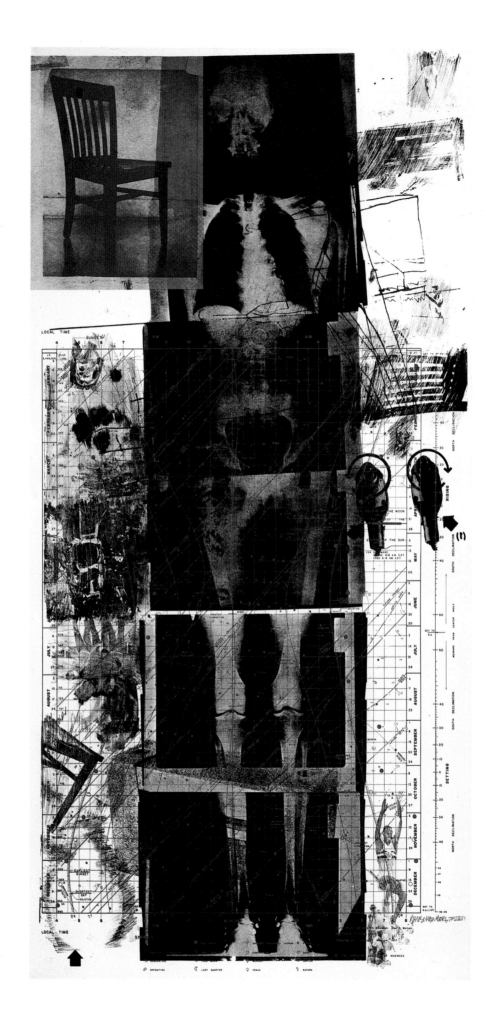

53. Jim Dine. *Four C Clamps*. 1962. Published by Universal Limited Art Editions. Lithograph, 11¼ x 18⅞″ (28.5 x 48.0 cm.)

54. Claes Oldenburg. *Tea Bag* from *Four on Plexiglas*. 1966. Published by Multiples, Inc. Silkscreen
on felt, clear Plexiglas, and plastic, 39⁵/₁₆ x 28¹/₁₆ x 3″ (99.8 x 71.3 x 7.6 cm.)

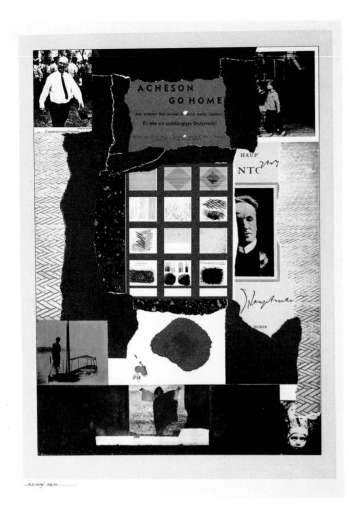

55. R. B. Kitaj. *Acheson Go Home*. 1963. Published by
Marlborough Gallery, London. Silkscreen, 28¾ x 21″
(73.0 x 53.4 cm.). The Museum of Modern Art, New
York, Dorothy Braude Edinburg Fund

56. Jim Dine. *Throat* from *11 Pop Artists*. 1965. Published by
Original Editions. Silkscreen, 30 x 24″ (76.2 x 61.0 cm.).
The Museum of Modern Art, New York, gift of Original
Editions

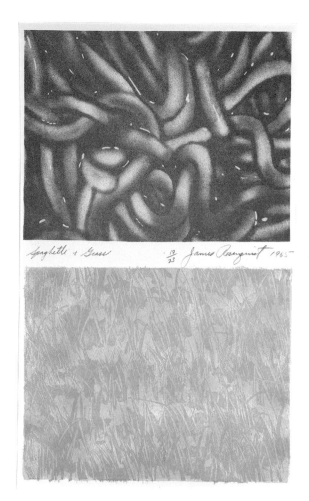

57. James Rosenquist. *Spaghetti and Grass.* 1965. Published by Universal Limited Art Editions. Lithograph, 27⅞ x 17⁵⁄₁₆″ (70.8 x 44.0 cm.). Courtesy Joseph and Eunice Fearer

58. James Rosenquist. *Flamingo Capsule.* 1973. Published by Multiples, Inc./Castelli Graphics. Lithograph and silkscreen, 26 x 68″ (71.2 x 172.6 cm.). Courtesy Maurice Sanchez

59. Roy Lichtenstein. *Reverie* from *11 Pop Artists*.
1965. Published by Original Editions. Silkscreen,
27⅛ x 22¹⁵/₁₆″ (68.9 x 58.2 cm.). Courtesy Judith
Goldberg

60. Robert Indiana. *LOVE*. 1967. Published by
Mass Art, Inc., and Multiples, Inc. Silkscreen,
34 x 34″ (86.4 x 86.4 cm.)

61. Roy Lichtenstein. *Cathedrals #2, #3*, and *#4*, from a series of six. 1969. Published by Gemini G.E.L. Lithographs, 41¹³⁄₁₆ x 27″ (106.2 x 68.6 cm.). © copyright Gemini G.E.L., Los Angeles, California, 1969

Describing his printed work of the late 1960s, Roy Lichtenstein said that his Art Deco–inspired works, such as *Peace through Chemistry*, were "a little like WPA murals," and that his *Cathedrals* "are meant to be manufactured Monets." Prior to his printmaking efforts at Gemini G.E.L. in 1969, Lichtenstein finished a group of paintings that were variations on two Monet themes (*Cathedrals* and *Haystacks*). He used the same view of Rheims cathedral for this series of six prints. Repeating Monet's plan of showing the transformation of the façade from dawn to dusk, Lichtenstein uses his familiar dot technique to indicate both the changing intensity and color of light and the structure of the building. Using only dots in primary colors the artist has further abstracted the subject, yet he retains the one effect that the Impressionist painter sought, the revelation of an object through the eye's perception of the organization of surface. In both cases, this occurs only after the viewer moves a sufficient distance from the picture. Unlike most of Lichtenstein's paintings and prints, the *Cathedrals* have no black lines to encompass the dots (which, up to this time, have represented continuous tone). His experiments with the value of dots alone later culminated in a series of prints and paintings based upon mirrors, in which lines, dots, and solid colors were used exclusively as indicators of form, shadow, and reflection. Subsequently, he returned to using black outlines around areas filled with one of a large repertoire of patterns that include his customary Ben Day dots.

62. Andy Warhol. *Jackie III* from *11 Pop Artists*. 1965. Published by Original Editions. Silkscreen, 39¾ x 29⅞" (101.0 x 76.0 cm.). Courtesy Castelli Graphics

63. OPPOSITE Andy Warhol. *Flowers*. 1970. Published by Factory Additions. Silkscreen, 36 x 36" (91.4 x 91.4 cm.). Courtesy of Castelli Graphics

In 1964 Warhol began to silkscreen a photograph of four flowers onto canvas, adding colors to the basic grainy black image by repeating the shapes of the flowers and rotating the screens containing only those shapes so that their printing would not necessarily coincide with the photographed flowers. Another screen was made to print an all-over color around the colored flower shapes. The result was an imperfectly decipherable image which exists on two levels: that of the photograph and that of the nearly abstract color shapes which, like water spots on a window, transform the details of what they transparently cover. Subsequently, Warhol had the screens made in several different sizes, exploiting the medium which made it possible for his assistants to print thirty-three canvases and over eight hundred paper impressions. These later, more or less ephemeral renditions of Warhol's most pleasant image, were executed at the Factory, his studio organized along commercial lines, where great quantities of printed work as well as movies were produced. The repetitive, boring work of the assembly line was taken up within an art context, cleverly embracing its philosophy more in the product than in the procedure (the Factory was known to be a rather casual and unpredictable environment). Finally, these *Flowers*, unlike the earlier, unlimited versions, were printed by a commercial silkscreen printer. The *Flowers* perfectly render the sort of stroboscopic, concentration-shattering view of objects that was a sensation of considerable popularity in the 1960s. As always, Warhol's selected theme is ultimately subversive, yet the set of ten *Flowers* issued in 1970 were framed and hung together on the fashionable stark white walls of many who fancied themselves supporters of contemporary art. Warhol exploited the tendency to acquire art for its fashionable clout, having been in the fashion business himself for many years creating advertisements that had a faintly decadent aura. Probably more than any of his contemporaries, Warhol reflected through a distorting mirror the society that supported contemporary art.

64. ABOVE Tom Wesselmann. *Nude Print*. 1969. Published by Chiron Press. Silkscreen, 16¹⁵⁄₁₆ x 23″ (43.0 x 58.4 cm.). The Museum of Modern Art, New York, gift of the artist

66. OPPOSITE Ernest Trova. Plate from *F. M. Manscapes*. 1969. Published by Pace Editions, Inc. Silkscreen, 23⅞ x 23⅞″ (60.6 x 60.6 cm.)

In the late 1960s, the sleek, polished metal sculptures of the St. Louis artist Ernest Trova appeared to fulfill the apprehensions of many humanists: machines had finally taken over. Trova's humanoids (not yet a patented word of science fiction) seemed to be the ultimate robots, apparently having lost all their physical functions or, rather, having had such functions replaced by wheels and other mechanical gadgets. These featureless figures were named by the artist *Falling Man*, probably less precisely a commentary on the human situation than on human movement through space. Related to the work of the English sculptor Edouardo Paolozzi, whose figures of a decade earlier were made up of cast machine parts and other assembly-line debris, Trova's sculptures went further into the realm of Pop Art by becoming themselves mechanical species. Trova's prints, all silkscreens, partake of the same sort of anonymous, machine-made character. In this work a series of "falling men" fan out like the blades of a jet motor. The hard edge for which stencil is best used makes the transitions of planes of colors take on an innocuous decorative value, absorbing the human element even further into a pattern. Borrowing the Art Deco form of Hollywood's Oscar statuette, Trova was one of the first post-war artists to allude to that decorative style, which began to return to popular interest in the 1970s.

65. Nicholas Krushenick. Untitled. 1965. Lithograph, 28⅞ x 16¹³⁄₁₆″ (73.4 x 43.0 cm.). University of New Mexico Art Museum

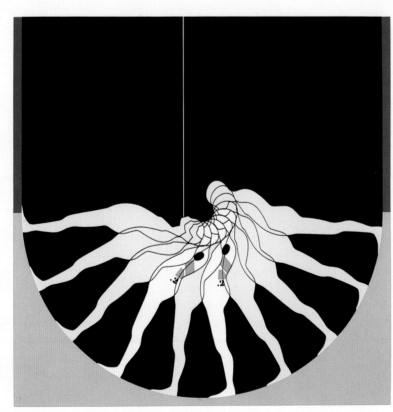

67. Lee Bontecou. *Fourth Stone*. 1963. Published by Universal Limited Art Editions. Color lithograph, 37^{15}/$_{16}$ x 29^{5}/$_{16}$″ (96.4 x 74.5 cm.)

While Marisol and Segal produced sculptures that evoked the same brash, disorienting view of the human predicament as the work of the Pop artists, several other sculptors were making equally provocative statements without depicting the human figure. Lee Bontecou's mammoth constructions of canvas stretched between segments of welded steel and attached to the frame with bits of copper wire were overpowering. They were made as wall-hanging pieces and loomed above and into space like strangely futuristic architecture that might have ominous functions. Bontecou's subject seems clarified somewhat in her prints, where swirling forms made of segments like the sculpture, often surrounding a black void, fill an ambiguous space. *Fourth Stone* (all her lithographs were titled numerically) shows these strange objects in a closed position, still floating, perhaps like planets, in a space articulated by bands. As with most sculptors' prints, the sense of objects in space is uppermost and at odds with the formalist motivations of contemporary painters. Nevertheless, in this print the strips that connect the orbs stretch out like so many rubber bands, flattening the sense of depth. These bands were created by pressing tape onto the stone, and using the residue of glue as the "drawing" when the stone was etched. In the late 1960s, Bontecou made sculptures from vacuum-formed, transparent plastic in the forms of fish and flowers, which she translated into a few lithographs. She made no prints during the 1970s, but returned to ULAE and began to work again in this medium in 1980.

68. Marisol. *Papagallo*. 1965. Published by Universal
Limited Art Editions. Lithograph, 16¹³⁄₁₆ x 11⅝″
(42.7 x 29.5 cm.)

69. George Segal. *Three Figures in Red Shirts: Two Front, One Back* from *Blue Jeans Series*. 1975. Published by 2 RC Editions.
Etching and aquatint, 38¹¹⁄₁₆ x 77¹⁵⁄₁₆″ (98.3 x 198.0 cm.)

70. H. C. Westermann. Plate from the portfolio *See America First*. 1968. Lithograph, 21¾ x 30¹⁄₁₆″ (55.3 x 76.3 cm.)

71. Edward Ruscha. *Standard Station*. 1966. Published by Audrey Sabol. Silkscreen, 25¾ x 40⅛″ (65.4 x 101.9 cm.). Brooke Alexander, Inc.

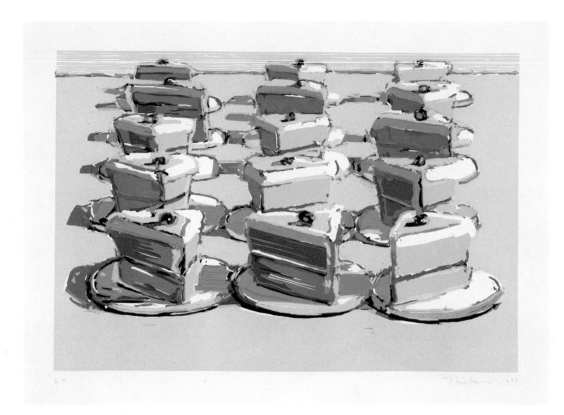

72. Wayne Thiebaud. *Boston Cremes*. 1970. Published by Parasol Press Ltd. Linoleum cut, 13⁹/₁₆ x 20⁵/₁₆" (34.4 x 51.6 cm.). The Museum of Modern Art, New York, John B. Turner Fund

A former advertising designer and art professor, Wayne Thiebaud brought his exceptional professional background and the palette of the Northern California and Bay Area artists (such as Diebenkorn) to illuminate his Pop style. Among the subjects that he painted during the early 1960s were edible items—pies, cakes, and lollipops—and women shown off guard in normal activities such as eating or sunbathing who were, nevertheless, treated uniformly like consumable objects. He made several etchings of his food images, which, despite the evident commercial sameness of the objects, are clearly no different from classical still-life compositions. In the linoleum cuts that he made with Arnera, Picasso's printer in Vallauris, the plastic quality that enlivens Thiebaud's paintings is translated into a glossy, enamel-like surface. When Claes Oldenburg presented his painted plaster cakes in a secondhand counter display case in 1962, he was mimicking a reality that had not yet been consciously perceived by the public. Thiebaud's pies clearly occupy the same area of reality but intensify our realization of how we have been deceived. Ultimately, the repetition of the same pie in regular rows becomes an abstraction. The process of printing one color at a time in isolated shapes is readily perceived in Thiebaud's composition, which never departs from its methodical, commercial-art formula.

CHAPTER FOUR

As provocative as the works of Pop Art were, they did not exist in a void. Non-figurative abstract styles persisted, and were generally considered somewhat more palatable. Strangely enough, abstraction in the visual arts had been far more provocative over a much longer period than the kind of genre art that one might associate with Pop, but in the late 1960s the dispassionate forms of geometric abstraction or the more psychologically involving swirls and strokes of Abstract Expressionism were soothing in comparison to the disturbing subjects served up by the Pop Artists.

Aware of American society's growing tendency to seek mechanical solutions to all kinds of problems, some artists attempted to improvise on scientifically grounded patterns as a way of expressing their realization of the reduction of human input. The works characterized as Op Art, for example, were often similar in form to the illustrations of certain theories of optics, or followed such theories to their practical conclusions by dwelling upon the simplest stimuli. The excitement engendered by many works of this type was more a product of successful discovery than of insight. Op Art was like fireworks and mirages melded together. It rather quickly came to be considered as vacuous as Pop by those who were looking for something more serious. Op Art compositions, however, were very suitable for printmaking. There was a large public pleasantly satisfied with an art form that gave nearly instantaneous recognition without being philosophically burdensome and that silently occupied its place on the wall until pointed out to perform its action of quick visual gratification once again. Significantly, Op Art was identified and became a popular form at the moment when it was discovered that some people actually sat and stared at their television sets while the test pattern was on. This pattern was usually made of close groups of lines that intersected the normal linear transmission of the TV picture. Interference created quite sophisticated variations on these patterns; there must have been many people who enjoyed "playing" with the patterns (or making their own Op Art).

The enjoyment of other forms of abstract art was personal and inimical to uniform interpretation, and therefore perfectly suited to the increasingly anti-social, reclusive older generation. The younger generation, still capable of widespread emotional response, spent its energies in communal lifestyles, group protests, inventing ways for their "cool" and remote elders to "get in touch" with their emotions, and so forth. While abstract styles from Abstract Expressionist to Minimalist were accepted relatively calmly, other forms that emerged from this disparity in response, such as Earth Art, Performance and Video Art, and Conceptual Art, were as far from most people's concept of "art" as the next galaxy. The moment had passed when imagination and other creative components dwelt upon the moon as an idealistic goal: it had become part of the "real world" in 1969.

The younger Abstract Expressionists—Sam Francis, Robert Motherwell, and Helen Frankenthaler—had found the key to printmaking early in the 1960s. Frankenthaler learned the craft by persistent practice at ULAE, where she produced about a dozen lithographs between 1961 and 1967. She turned to etching in 1967 (when Tatyana Grosman received a grant from the National Endowment for the Arts to build an etching workshop) and continued to make prints in that medium at ULAE until 1974. Her first lithographs were made with tentative, heavily laden brush marks, but in subsequent prints she found ways in which to reproduce the washes that characterized her stained canvases (Fig. 73). The calm, dreamlike interiors of her compositions, punctured and vitalized by shots of brightly colored lines, were beautifully interpreted in washes of tusche or pale sheets of aquatint. As it did for several artists, aquatint provided Frankenthaler with a fresh and appealing medium for abstract art. Aquatint differed from lithography or silkscreen in that its continuous texture was actually composed of minute and dimensional dots whose surfaces reflected light instead of absorbing it. Color aquatint, therefore, was more colorful while still transformable into paler and darker intensities. Frankenthaler and Motherwell both took advantage of this medium to enliven their compositions of the late 1960s, and in prints such as *Weather Vane* and *Lilac Arbor* Frankenthaler displayed great sensitivity to its use.

Her most important contribution to the development of printmaking in this period, however, was her work in woodcut. In the early 1970s there was renewed interest in the printed work of the great Norwegian artist Edvard Munch. Of all the turn-of-the-century artists it was Munch who made the greatest contribution to the history of printmaking, particularly through his woodcuts, which were an inspiration to the German Expressionists. He often used an interesting technique in his woodcuts—cutting out the forms with a band saw, inking them individually, and placing them together for printing—which Frankenthaler perceived as a possible method for her own compositions. In *East and Beyond* (1973) and *Savage Breeze* (1974) she found the perfect way to emulate the ink-soaked cloth of her paintings by lightly inking and wiping large, textured sheets of wood. She cut through the wood and inserted pieces of harder wood to introduce the staccato interruptions that she desired.

Like other contemporary printmakers, Frankenthaler recognized the role that paper played in her work. In her most successful woodcut, *Essence Mulberry*, made with Ken Tyler in 1977 (Fig. 74), she designed the printed area to cover only one half of the paper surface, incorporating the unusual color and texture of the paper into the total composition. Less engrossed in the printmaking process than Francis or Motherwell, Frankenthaler has worked with Tyler and Kathan Brown of Crown Point Press in Oakland, California, producing perhaps a dozen prints in as many years.

Robert Motherwell worked at ULAE during its early days and returned in 1968 after an absence of six years to begin his major work there: a large portfolio-book, *A la pintura*, designed around the text of Raphael Alberti. This series of twenty-one aquatints conjoined with lines of text is a tour de force of graphic design and sublime printmaking. Motherwell found the perfect means of presenting his forms in the intense blacks and radiant colors of the medium, and his "open" compositions, in which three lines of a rectangle descend into a large, oblong color field, were particularly successful. The undisturbed field of aquatint (modulated on occasion, but not to the point of disrupting the perception of continuity) was in sharp contrast with the passionate lines that interrupted it.

In the following decade Motherwell created many lithographs with Ken Tyler (both before and after the printer left Gemini in 1974 to set up his own workshop in Bedford Village, New York, quite near Motherwell's Connecticut home) and also made aquatints in his own studio (Fig. 75). By 1980 he had produced nearly two hundred and fifty prints over the years since his tentative experiments in Hayter's workshop in 1942.

Francis, too, continued to make lithographs throughout the 1960s and '70s, mainly in Los Angeles, at Tamarind (1963 and 1969) and at Gemini beginning in 1971. He also had his own press, but he never significantly changed the style of printmaking he developed in Switzerland in 1960. One area which Francis seems to have found attractive has been the move away from uniform, mechanically perfect editions. He and Garner Tullis—whose International Institute for Experimental Printmaking, in central California, was essentially a place where artists could work with paper pulp—made some monotypes mixed with other materials and created simultaneously with the paper foundation. Peripheral to actual printmaking, Francis's work of this type nevertheless does include printing and is representative of the increasing tendency toward craft or handmade materials that entered the mainstream of printmaking activity during the 1970s. Francis and several other artists turned to monotype, papermaking, and other unique methods that depended upon the use of a printshop. Because they were famous enough to remain acceptable no matter what materials they used, there was little criticism of the transformation. One might think that these techniques developed because there were too many editions of prints around and not enough drawings and paintings to fulfill the collectors' desire for the unique; but this was not the case. The truth seems to be that the print market was so well established and prints had such a high recognition factor that new materials introduced there were more readily accepted than elsewhere.

When optical or retinal art was canonized in 1965, several artists were grouped together whose work had much in common, primarily the preference to paint "flat." The colors they used had no modulations and followed paths, usually geometric in form, from one end of the picture plane to the other. Josef Albers's work was meant to exercise the eye by using a limited set of forms and colors. It was a mechanically oriented art, pleasing in its evidently simple but perplexing effect. His *Homage to the Square* prints in particular fulfilled the wishes of those who would have art that was "seen but not heard."

The series of paintings called *Homage to the Square* was begun around 1951 and evolved into prints in 1962. At first Albers provided only mechanical plans with indications of the colors to be used, which were then turned into silkscreen prints. At Tamarind in 1963, he learned more about printmaking, and began to experiment with densities of ink in order to create the sensations of aura and transference that were produced by his compositions of concentric squares. He continued making prints with Ken Tyler (who had been the master printer at Tamarind), first at Gemini, where in 1966 he made *White Line Squares*—a bravura effort that kept a vital straight line unprinted in the midst of some quite wonderful combinations of flatly printed colors—and in the 1970s at Tyler Graphics. Albers moved back into silkscreen which, through Tyler's experimentation with photo-transfers, developed into a series titled *Gray Instrumentations*, the surfaces of which looked truly satiny and photographic.

Albers was, of course, a living representative of the Bauhaus philosophy, but other artists, much younger than he, followed similar paths. Ad Reinhardt, associated with the Abstract Expressionists because of his age, similar interests, and occasional friendships, was one of the few painters of his generation to have served in World War II, thus missing the incubating situation that prevailed in New York during the early 1940s. He began to paint in fields of flat color in 1953. The nearly invisible contrasts between his colors, applied in wide, intersecting bands, had a peaceful but engrossing effect. Although he made a few prints, notably an album of silkscreens issued in 1966 (Fig. 80), Reinhardt could never obtain sufficient subtlety in the contrasting printed bands, and apparently considered all his prints disasters. Moreover, as his prints all relate to his black on black paintings, they were not very visible under the glass that was needed to protect their fragile surfaces.

Far more successful were the works of Ellsworth Kelly, who went to Paris in 1948 to study under the G.I. Bill, and returned to America in 1954 to make flat, colorful paintings that profited from his love for Matisse and Léger. Like Sam Francis, who lived in France from 1950 to 1957, he made his first lithographs abroad, in conjunction with a one-man show at Galerie Maeght in Paris in 1964 (Fig. 81). Kelly treated his lithographs as sets of color variants on compositions made up of two or three simple shapes. With perfectly flat, bright inks, Kelly obtained diverse effects. When one shape was contained within another of a contrasting color, their vibrations created a pleasant kinetic effect. The simple, rounded forms seemed to float free of the white paper upon which they were printed. After this group of twenty-seven lithographs and a series, nearly as large, of linear black and white drawings of plants, Kelly began to make prints in America, first with Hollander in New York and in 1970 at Gemini. Although his art demanded the bright hues that had so appealed to him in Matisse's cut-paper collages (some of which were made into the famous stencil prints for the book *Jazz*), Kelly usually preferred the inks of lithography to the granular, surface-oriented paints of the stencil process, silkscreen. Through the juxtaposition of exactly the right inks, usually close to complementary, within geometric forms that relied, like his shaped canvases and sculptures, on a white background or void for definition, his prints presented the ideal abstraction of form and color in a gratifyingly undisturbing balance. Kelly continued to work at Gemini into the 1970s, creating a few silkscreens and a set of black and white embossed prints (Fig. 82). He also turned to handmade paper works under the direction of Ken Tyler, who developed a mold into which Kelly could put a substantial amount of dyed pulp, thereby obtaining his distinctive, large shapes.

The use of contrasting colors flatly applied was not Kelly's exclusive domain, however. Other artists at the edge of expressionism, such as Alexander Liberman, also produced prints (Fig. 83) that, like their works in other mediums, depended upon sharp-edged form and nearly mechanical application of tone (Liberman's sculpture was also treated in this manner, and often recalled the exposed pipes and structural elements that architects of the 1960s painted in colors that made their separate functions recognizable). This use of contrasting colors connected these artists with Op Art in the mind of the public, although the ideas expressed in their works were more scrupulously to be identified as color field art, and led directly to the most succinct and refined manifestation of the tendency, Minimalism.

Richard Anuszkiewicz and Frank Stella are two artists whose work clearly shows how similar compositional elements were organized for different emphasis and effect. In his paintings and silkscreen prints Anuszkiewicz often used concentrically arranged parallel lines to produce, through modulating color, optical vibrations of vertiginous power. The prints that decorate a volume of William Blake's poetry, *Inward Eye* (1970, Fig. 85), demonstrate how bands of closely allied hues can produce the effect of movement, yet have a delicate serenity induced by the concentrated, singular idea behind the work. The artists who sought to obtain effects emanating from color juxtapositions or linear arrangements were creating an abstract version of trompe-l'oeil art. Still, it was not possible to make the eye see something move that was actually completely static without understanding some of the principles that caused this error of optical judgment. The Op Artists were examining through their art the process of seeing; the color field artists and Minimalists were examining the process of making art itself. In both instances, lasting changes in the perception of art were the result.

Frank Stella's early paintings were concentric bands of one color, not sharply defined, but insistent upon their formal control of the entire canvas. Following some of the ideas that Jasper Johns pursued in his paintings of flags and targets, Stella sought to go even further in the presentation of the flat, patterned composition that emphasized the shape of the support. He made the contours of his canvas follow his image so that there would be no doubt that the shaped canvas on the wall was exactly that and not a "picture" of something. The constructs of printmaking were not so easily changed. Stella's earliest prints at Gemini were sets of compositions consisting of flat groupings of parallel bands, each placed upon an undisturbed white surface, or in some prints, on graph paper. He was seeking a way to produce in print the same object-to-background relationship he had achieved in his canvases. By 1970 he had completed a series of paintings based on bands drawn with a protractor, generally following the shape of the half-circle and using extremely bright colors (as opposed to the metallic or subdued tones of his earlier works). Between 1970 and

1974 he produced several very large lithographs and silkscreens in this mode, as well as a series titled *Eccentric Polygons* after an earlier group of paintings.

Stella liked to make a series of works on a single formal subject. He began modestly with small albums of prints, intending eventually to render most of his series of paintings into printed form. Although he produced one or two prints that were not part of this program, he was still returning to older series of paintings for his print images when he made his first offset lithographs, based on *Concentric Squares* and *Mitered Mazes*, for Petersburg Press in 1972–73. Among these unusual, colored-crayon prints is *Jasper's Dilemma* (Fig. 86), two concentric squares side by side, one in bright color, the other in varieties of gray, a direct reference to Johns's work of 1963—now a decade removed from its unmistakably influential advent.

Noteworthy from a technical standpoint is the almost simultaneous discovery of offset lithography by both Stella and Johns. The use of an offset proofing press, where the plate or stone remained flat while the inked image was first picked up from its surface by a roller and then deposited on the paper, allowed the artist to work without taking into consideration the reversal of the image (as in regular lithography and etching, although not in silkscreen). The deposit of ink upon the surface of the paper was usually less dense, so special inks were developed by printers to give more substance to the printed image which, as with silkscreen, was laid upon the paper rather than being pressed into it. Printing was easier and consequently faster, so that the artist was able to work with more concentrated attention to the evolution of the print itself.

Some of the abstract artists preferred an arrangement of material that was less rigidly formal than Stella's, although they still emphasized that element over all others. For a short while such art was referred to as Lyric Abstraction. Its pleasant colors and softer patterns were much admired. On the East Coast, Jules Olitski created paintings and a few prints of mottled colors spread across the entire plane, interrupted at one edge by an intrusion of another similarly handled color. His was essentially a painterly style; its transition to silkscreen and lithography was imperfect (Fig. 88). Far more successful was the work of the West Coast artist Ed Moses, whose first prints were cut-out lithographs, folded and linear, related to Op Art. These were made at Tamarind, but later prints produced at Cirrus Editions (an adventurous enterprise founded in 1970 by a Tamarind printer, Jean R. Milant) were filled with airy, pastel color patterns that were indeed lyrical (Fig. 89). Moses's best prints were layers of tissue upon which his bars and dashes were printed in transparent, delicate tones. This fairly romantic tendency derived its impetus somewhat from the works of Morris Louis (who had died in 1962) and Kenneth Noland (another G.I. Bill artist who studied in Paris), whose patterned, stained canvases were the most notable pairing of the geometric with the lyrical.

Noland was not interested in printmaking per se (his few silkscreens are more or less exact reproductions of his paintings), but in the late 1970s he found a suitable medium for multiple works in handmade paper, first with Tullis in California and later with Tyler in Bedford Village. Like Kelly, Noland used a method that isolated sections of colored paper pulp, thereby producing nearly identical compositions, even if the colors and their densities varied (Fig. 90).

A stronger movement, closer in philosophy and ambition to those abstract tendencies described earlier, was Minimalism, the attempt to reach the most succinct, vital meaning of two- or three-dimensional art. Minimalism had to co-exist with its sibling, Conceptual Art. Artists of both movements sought the meaning of art through analysis of its elements. Many names were given to branches of this examination and its products, because there was no moment at which one could be ferreted out and identified as *the* current style. The pluralism forecast by the futurists was at hand; it manifested itself by ridding art of the concept of the avant-garde.

To the Minimalists, art was purest when it was stripped down to its essentials. Thus, the white paintings of Malevich, rooted in the Suprematist expression of the early twentieth century, found a follower in Robert Ryman. His white compositions, both in paint and in print, emulate this earlier radical form, but also take advantage of the accumulated awareness of the contemporary viewer, who is able to recognize the subtle signs by which Ryman activates the surface of the pure white paint or ink, and to perceive the unexpected ways in which that white approaches the edge of the canvas or plate. In this sort of minimal statement, the complex balance of geometric forms that had been the central composing formula of abstract art was replaced by a single fundamental element that, extracted from the rest, still had sufficient beauty and integrity to satisfy.

Among the other Minimalists who made prints were Robert Mangold and Brice Marden. Both were painters of flat, subtly toned canvases that were consciously shaped, Mangold using untraditional geometric forms such as triangles and half-circles and Marden painting two or more rectangles in closely allied hues edge to edge to form one composition. Ryman, Mangold, and Marden were brought to Crown Point Press by Robert Feldman, the founder of Parasol Press (which was named after the sign of an umbrella maker which hung on the building Feldman occupied). Kathan Brown, the young intaglio printmaker who ran Crown Point, was able to produce unsurpassably pure passages of aquatint that gave her artists a surface of sufficient liveliness without complicating their limited statement. Brown helped the three Minimalists create prints of sublime simplicity and magic (Figs. 91, 92, 93). Marden chose to work solely in black and white, placing large, daunting black rectangles next to outlined blank spaces. These prints, made for the most part between 1971 and 1973, had an isolated precedent in Barnett Newman's last two prints, done in 1969, which were black aquatint bands upon an uninked rectangular plate (Fig. 94). From a technical standpoint alone there was a vast difference between Newman's intense but unevenly etched black band and what Brown was able to accomplish for artists who would accept modulation only if they could control the way it disturbed the surface.

Dorothea Rockburne also produced a set of prints at Crown Point Press through a commission from Parasol (which, unlike ULAE, Gemini, and all the other printer-publishers mentioned so far, was exclusively a publisher, and had to develop or utilize printers and presses that could provide both the desired medium and supporting atmosphere required by each project and artist). Rockburne had long before discarded the tradition of stretched canvas as a basis for painting and had taken the canvas itself and folded it into geometric forms derived from the mathematical relationship known as the "golden section." Her printing project was complex and unconventional: each sheet was first printed with thin, short gray lines, barely visible, which indicated where the paper was to be folded; the paper was folded and printed again with white aquatint which produced slightly perceptible tonal and textural changes in the paper; the paper was then unfolded, but because of its rather stiff composition retained the creases so that each print was actually a relief (Fig. 96). Rockburne was not the first artist to fold paper nor to print it in such an unorthodox fashion, but she, like many of her contemporaries, saw her project as a series of processes following an exact mathematical formula. Like them, she felt that the success of her works had to be based on the perfection of both the formulae and the execution.

But the primary representative of this theoretical bent was Sol LeWitt. His work is the most perfect example of the irrelevance of stylistic labels. He thought of his work as Conceptual in that he began with a formula (lines straight, in four directions, in four colors, etc.) which he then stringently followed to produce a physical representation of a minimal statement about art. The realization of his concepts, often accomplished by assistants following his concise and logically simple instructions, was equally important to their success.

In 1970 LeWitt was associated with Virginia Dwan, a Los Angeles dealer who moved to New York at that time. Her gallery represented many of the younger artists whose work was often radically different from the predictable painting of the moment. LeWitt, for example, produced large cubes covered with penciled lines, or drew such lines over an entire wall. Like many of the Dwan artists, LeWitt found no sense in confining his essentially graphic art to unique pieces, so that well before he began to make etchings in 1971, he was producing silkscreens for Sarah Lawrence Press in 1970 (Fig. 97), as well as unlimited editions of offset prints and books that were available at very small cost to all who wished to have them.

Behind LeWitt's work of this period lies the principle followed by many of his generation: art should no longer be elitist; it should exist as universally as possible (in books, in unrestricted excavated areas of land transformed into man-made works of non-functional beauty, in free performances); and it should not be in any way precious. By providing instructions for his wall drawings and other works, LeWitt made it possible for anyone to reproduce them. His etchings, however, led to something else, since the plates were all drawn by him. Ultimately, the medium itself seemed to insist that he return to the role of craftsman and revel in the luxurious perfection of his work. The process of making fine prints, which required considerable investment of time, manpower, and materials, all of which finally cost money, was a temptation that many artists whose moral philosophies were at odds with the "system" could not resist. From 1971 to 1983 LeWitt made over three hundred etchings at Crown Point, usually in series of plates following finite systems, which were meant either to be shown together or bound into books. In some cases only two or three copies of these prints were made, the costs being prohibitive (Fig. 98).

The sculptor Donald Judd was another artist who revealed little more than the process by which the work was formed. In 1961 he made some minimal wall sculptures of building lumber, untrimmed and glued or nailed together in parallel strips, diagonally trimmed at top and bottom. Eight years later he used these as printing forms, applying red or blue paint to transfer the image to paper (Fig. 100).

In 1977 and 1978 Michael Heizer, who created environmental sculpture by moving mammoth areas of land, cut some scratched metal plates into geometric forms that related to each other either as portions of a whole or as quantitative equivalents of a larger mass, and printed them as if they were etchings. These impressions of randomly marked plates in compositions that were governed by logical formulae display in the clearest way possible the duality of artistic expression prevalent in the 1970s: on the one hand, abdication of complete control over materials by allowing them to be the organizing factor in the physicality of the artwork; on the other hand, affirmation of the beauty of logic and man's control over the organization of thought (Fig. 101).

The concepts of game theory and chance—an interlocking of premeditated procedures based on perceived limitations and their unpredictable outcome—were now common though rather intimidating subjects for art. Among the older artists who had made references in their work to numerical sequences and chance theories were Alfred Jensen and the composer John Cage. The precursor of chance art, Cage was a romantic at heart. Since his days at Black Mountain College in the 1940s and early 1950s, he had affected the creative thinking of many artists by his attitude toward his own medium. His concept of music was that it could not be separated from all sound; his idea that composition should be constructed upon the same basis of chance as life influenced Rauschenberg and Johns, and later became a visual art form for Cage himself. Taking the I Ching as a procedure, Cage provided himself with a sequence of words from a poem, for example, added other factors such as type size and color, and cast them like so many dice into a plan for his compositions. His first work was a multiple, a set of Plexiglas sheets standing in a frame like Rauschenberg's earlier *Shades*, called *Plexigram* (1969). The elements were also used the same year for a print on black paper, *Not Wanting to Say Anything About Marcel* (Fig. 104). With the encouragement of Kathan Brown, Cage became even more involved in printmaking in the 1970s, and has created dozens of etchings with images borrowed from chosen sources and arranged in I Ching–generated compositions. Cage's choice of pastel colors has lent his work a soft and rather whimsical air, giving the systematic conception of his works a visual beauty akin to that which mathematicians often perceive in the results of their equations.

Alfred Jensen made only a few lithographs, in *1¢ Life* in 1964, and a set at Tamarind titled *A Pythagorean Notebook* in 1965 (Fig. 102). His blocks of color and written explanations provided sequential codified compositions which may have served as examples to LeWitt and to an even younger artist, Mel Bochner. The latter concentrated upon the games aspect of logical theories; in his prints he set up the elements of a game in which the theoretical result is crystal clear. The diagrammatical nature of his elegant aquatints had a familiar reference to learning experiences that extended their appreciation. Eventually his art became more geometric, and overlays of triangular planes in a spectrum of colors revealed the romantic aspect of the theoretician's art (Fig. 105).

In 1961 Shusaku Arakawa moved to America from Japan. His large, colorful prints concisely characterize the atmosphere of the commercial sector in the later 1970s, when some artists were encouraged to produce works which were, for the most part, printed counterparts of their paintings. In homage to Jasper Johns, Arakawa used Johns's stencil lettering as a formal element in his paintings and prints, which were codified into philosophical statements about the nature of seeing, creating, and other fundamental concepts, that he and his wife, the poet Madeline Gins, brought together under the general title *The Mechanism of Meaning*. The prints have a special quality that is rarely encountered in this sort of artistic pronouncement: consummate craftsmanship and understanding of technique. Arakawa has shown considerable bravado in combining various mediums in prints such as *That in Which* (1979), but the essential components of his visual statements are given their greatest clarity in etching (Fig. 106).

Johns himself had, by the 1970s, developed his style of cross-hatchings in repeatable panels and was using print techniques to create subtle nuances of line, color, and even form. Few artists could "repeat" themselves in so creative a manner, and the abundance of prints Johns has produced in this mode, highly structured and intellectual, although ostensibly just a pattern of lines of varying lengths that extend from edge to edge, reveal that the thesis upon which his early work was developed provided the foundation for many of the stylistic modes of subsequent decades (Fig. 107).

One of the movements that explored ideas about the nature of two-dimensional art and visual meaning was Photorealism, which flourished on both sides of the Atlantic. The Photorealists presented figurative work within the constructs of art as an abstract planar form, by using the imagery produced by the camera with its single lens rather than the binocular understanding of space developed in Renaissance painting, that is, perspective. This is not to say that the works of Richard Estes, views of city shops and buildings without any human presence, do not show that some objects are farther away than others, but the conscious attempt to produce an illusion of perspective is secondary to the procession of lines, colors, and patterns from one edge of the composition to the other. Even the reflections in the windows are treated in the same way, incorporated into the skin of a depthless reality (Fig. 108).

The same principles apply to Alex Katz's portraits of his wife, friends, and dog. Flat, bland faces, evenly illuminated so that all sense of modeling is eliminated, gaze from the silkscreens and aquatints he made in the 1970s. Katz has preferred that his printers copy onto screens and plates the essential outlines of his compositions, taken from his paintings or drawings. When the proofing begins Katz works directly with the printing materials, transforming what was a reproduction into a print. Balancing the colors, strength of lines, and other details, he reveals the correct character of each work for its printed form (Fig. 109).

Chuck Close is more concerned than Katz with the principles of photographic reproduction when he creates portraits. Working from a photograph with a shallow depth of field, Close divides his canvas into a grid which he then fills in, in some works with airbrush, in some others with fingerprints, eventually and arduously producing gigantic portraits. In his first print he applied the same method to mezzotint. Subsequently he did lithographs and etchings, small, wiggling lines filling the squares in quantities varying according to the desired darkness of the area. The dots of photo-mechanical reproduction, which produce the gray tones between unprinted white and totally inked black, are the model for Close's method. The painstaking labor of methodically filling each square with the proper number of lines or inked fingerprints produces works that emphasize the phenomenon of visual acuity, the artificial depth of field occurring within the portrait, so that part of the skin is microscopically sharp and other, nearer or more distant sections are blurred (Fig. 110).

The most prolific of the painters who carried their figurative work in the formalist tradition into print has been Philip Pearlstein. He chooses to view his sprawling nudes from awkward angles, and mercilessly amputates heads and feet as he limits that viewpoint. Intricately patterned rugs and regularly laid-out floors surround nude flesh that is given some vestige of modeling through a structured method of shading (Fig. 111). Neutral forms that seem to resolve into human flesh in some compositions appear again in mammoth landscapes. With little variation of color, Pearlstein's aquatints *Downtown Manhattan*, *The Sphinx*, and *Machu Picchu* present a completely lifeless world, and confirm the abstract nature even of his nudes.

One of the first artists to merge elements of figuration with the surface of the work without alluding to volume or depth was John Clem Clarke. His prints included airbrush renditions of paintings by Rigaud and Chardin, and more abstract patterns of greatly enlarged brushstrokes that related to the concurrent style of Lyric Abstraction, in which the pattern itself became the subject (Fig. 112).

There were a few artists whose prints borrowed the regularized forms of repetitious design. Such work, reflecting as it inevitably does the tedious labor of traditional handwork such as quilting, seemed to be a predictable mode of emerging feminist artists. Indeed, the accumulation of decorative forms has its pioneer model in the sculptures of Louise Nevelson. Although she made quite a few etchings at Atelier 17 in the early 1950s, the prints that more closely parallel her sculptures of glued-together sticks, dowels, and other discarded decorative woodwork are the collage-like lithographs done at Tamarind in 1967 and the intaglio prints issued by Pace Graphics in the 1970s. Her print materials are net and lace, casually connecting geometric elements (Fig. 113).

The patterns of tiles in the lithographs of Joyce Kozloff, on the other hand, follow the same formal application as the works of the Minimalists (Fig. 114). Kozloff used her prints as wallpaper, producing a decorative environment from the sheets of printed paper and additional materials. Taking prints out of their protective frames was a typical 1970s act, part of the prevalent attempt to diminish if not destroy the preciousness of the art object. Many other artists made pattern paintings, but few turned to the print medium, even though there was a popular following in Europe for the American painters of this mode. A pleasant escape from the dry intellectualism of Minimalism, pattern art might be seen as a last-ditch effort to retain the formalist statement in two-dimensional art.

Certain examples of Conceptual Art reveal that pattern-making is merely another way of creating diagrams. The maps of Robert Morris, *Earth Projects* (1969), which were meant to stimulate deductive reasoning through visual information, may also be viewed simply as lines and color in a repetitive structure (Fig. 115). This earliest reference to environmental art in print form appears to state that the essential qualities of art can be found in untraditional subjects. The works of Morris and others who chose to present, rather than represent, their ideas were the most radical artistic phenomenon of the 1960s. The period of the Vietnam War differed from that of the Korean conflict nearly two decades earlier by virtue of the heightened sensitivity to ethics and political morality that was aroused by the deluge of information. The enormous cultural establishment that mushroomed during the early 1960s was perceived by many artists as sharing with other well-financed and highly organized areas of society a corrupt, deceitful, and unjust influence. Angrily seeking expression, they turned to public spaces in which to produce their messages. Morris's plans for vast, sculpted areas of land or one-time events taking place in remote, unpopulated terrains paralleled Robert Smithson's actual works, such as *Spiral Jetty*, for which photographs of the transformed landmass had to serve most people as the sole evocation of the artwork.

Christo, the Bulgarian-born artist whose work consisted of actions culminating in the enveloping in cloth of a building or landscape, combined several ideas that were of concern to many at the time: confrontation with the system (political and social), community action (the projects depended upon the labor of many volunteers), and transformation of the expected and ordinary into art. Christo sold drawings and prints of his projects to finance them. In 1971 he produced a portfolio of prints of unrealized projects that suitably confronted the cultural establishment: the wrapped and consequently inoperative Museum of Modern Art and Whitney Museum of American Art (Fig. 116).

Relying on the instantaneous recognition of TV imagery to convey his message—that pictures could mislead—Les Levine, an Irish-born Canadian, made several sets of prints in New York in the 1970s. He created many video works and therefore had an excellent understanding of how the linear format and visual trickery of faster-than-the-eye-can-see electronics could be manipulated in print (Fig. 119). Performance was the springboard for this sort of printed imagery: photographs of Levine in his own video performances; of Bruce Nauman's grimaces, the material for a series of holograms (Fig. 118); of Otto Piene's grandiose outdoor fire and air show at Massachusetts Institute of Technology (Fig. 120). Occasionally a subtly comfortable insertion of familiar handwork enhanced the often political message.

Vito Acconci, whose autoerotic performances usually occurred within an area occupied by an audience but out of its sight, made a few books with directions for his own performances, and prints that present the basic confrontation with commonly accepted mores in the more complacent context of the static visual image. His prints of pistols and penises annoyingly insinuated these forbidden images into the august domain of fine art. On the other hand, his series *Stones for a Wall* (1977) more gently permits a growing realization of horrible incursions into daily life (Fig. 121).

Prints as art for a wide public now became vehicles of public opposition. Hans Haacke, a German artist whose works were pointedly anti-establishment, had made simple, abstract embossed prints before he came to America. In the 1970s he conducted surveys that focused upon personal and corporate power and reached conclusions about its misuse. The few objects resulting from these projects have been prints and multiples that are abrasive in their luxurious, elegant presentation of the self-condemning statements and boasts of their subjects.

Other artistic forms that similarly made little contact with collectors were those Conceptual works utilizing only words. Significantly, the Conceptualists sincerely wished to remove the acquisitive, social–identity–verifying aspect from works of art. Through writing that evoked visual ideas, awareness of space and time factors in movement, stasis, and nearly any aspect of experience that could induce an image, they denied the precious, elitist values that they felt misrepresented the true expression of the artist. Printed in unlimited editions, the works of Joseph Kosuth and many others represent an important manifestation of art in print, although it would be contradictory to illustrate them in this volume. In many cases Conceptual Artists made use of imagery, often diagrams and photographs. These works usually depend on sequential observation and would be equally misrepresented as single illustrations. The books and booklets of West Coast artists Ed Ruscha and John Baldessari are typical examples of this genre.

The disintegration of the print as a pleasant picture was at the same time a re-integration of the print medium with its time-honored purpose of disseminating visual information. Rauschenberg's prints, for example, contained evidence of the social dilemma in his choice of photographs for his collage compositions, yet they also reflected the positive, hopeful spirit of the space explorations and the public's new awareness of the environment. Even though the tremendous variety of artistic concerns during the 1970s was seen by many as a dissolution of the strong character of American art, there was an ever-widening appreciation of prints, which, more conveniently than other mediums, communicated these diverse expressions.

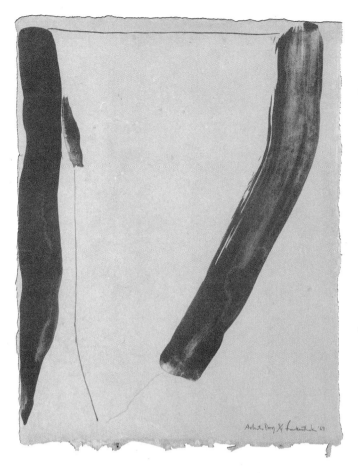

73. Helen Frankenthaler. *A Slice of the Stone Itself.*
1969. Published by Universal Limited Art Editions.
Lithograph, 18 x 14⅛″ (45.7 x 36.0 cm.)

74. Helen Frankenthaler. *Essence Mulberry.* 1977. Printed and
published by Tyler Graphics Ltd. Woodcut, 25 x 18⅞″
(63.5 x 47.9 cm.). © copyright Helen Frankenthaler/Tyler
Graphics Ltd. 1977

75. Robert Motherwell. Untitled. 1975. Aquatint, 12 x 10″ (30.5 x 25.5 cm.). Brooke Alexander, Inc.

11/23 (767

76. Cy Twombly. Untitled II. 1967–74. Published by Universal Limited Art Editions. Etching and aquatint, 23⅝ x 28⅛″ (60.0 x 71.4 cm.). Brooke Alexander, Inc.

The painter Cy Twombly developed as an artist at the same time as his friend Robert Rauschenberg; they were at Black Mountain College together in 1951. However, Twombly developed a more abstract form of expression, rarely introducing objects into his work as Rauschenberg did. In 1957 Twombly moved to Italy, and while he remains closely identified with American art, he has tended to incorporate the influences of his surroundings, especially the historical atmosphere of ancient Roman and classical tradition, into his art. Not a prolific printmaker, Twombly has made several series of prints and only a few single examples that repeat the compulsive calligraphic jottings that dart through his canvases and drawings. This print is one of two large plates that he made after a casual visit to Universal Limited Art Editions with Rauschenberg during the summer of 1967. Within two months he had etched a group of four small compositions and created a sort of sketchbook of drypoints. But Twombly was not familiar with the techniques of intaglio—the small plates were attempts to find a comfortable means of conveying his distinctive, spontaneous marks—and none of them displays the powerful gesture and texture of this aquatint. It seems clear that Twombly accomplished his goal despite his lack of technique, for the liquid flow of line emerging from the granular surface would be extremely difficult to replicate accurately.

77. Richard Diebenkorn. *Large Bright Blue*. 1980. Published by Crown Point Press. Etching and aquatint, 24 x 14⅜″ (61.0 x 36.5 cm.). Crown Point Press, Oakland, California, and New York, New York

Of all the artists who studied and worked in the Bay Area of California, Richard Diebenkorn has best maintained the fresh, clear atmosphere that has characterized both the representative and abstract art of that part of America. Having passed from painting in the Abstract Expressionist style to figurative subjects during the 1950s, Diebenkorn turned away from depicting recognizable objects in the late 1960s. This large aquatint derives from the landscape-based compositions, often shorelines, that have dominated his paintings since that time. Evocative of some of the more abstract works of Henri Matisse and sharing their predominance of blue tones, this print simply states the structure of a long, nearly infinite vista. The indefinite nature of the composition, unlike purely non-objective abstraction, still preserves the essence of a scenic representation. While Diebenkorn has given some works in this style titles that refer to specific places, the titles of this and other prints in this series (*Eight Color Etchings*) show rather his desire to declare his intentions. Designating some of the prints in the series as "constructs," Diebenkorn has approached each plate in a formal way, working through a set of essentially graphic forms. This print is one of two works having one plate in common: the one printed in blue. Fully inked, the plate was first used to print *Large Bright Blue* (in which the overall color appears in its undiluted brilliance). Still containing a residue of the blue ink, the plate was printed again (with only a tiny detail re-inked) on the print, *Large Light Blue*. The watery veil of color is a result of the process Diebenkorn used to create the plate, by painting with acid directly on an aquatint ground.

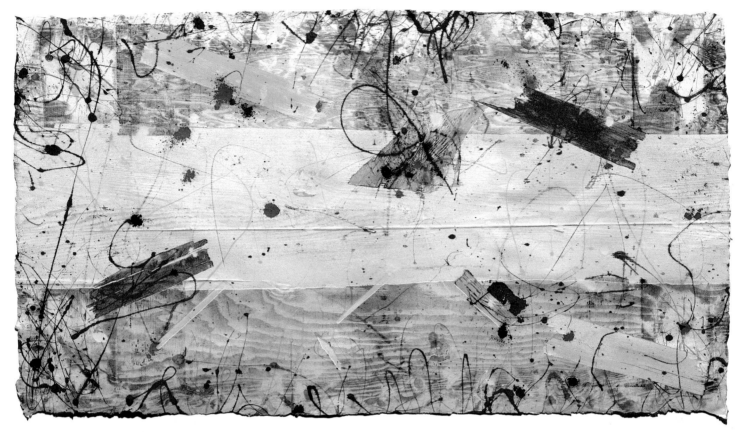

78. Sam Francis. Untitled. 1982. Monotype, 42 x 78″ (106.7 x 198.1 cm.). Courtesy Experimental Printmaking, San Francisco

79. Josef Albers. Plate V from *Homage to the Square: Midnight and Noon*. 1964. Lithograph, 15¾ x 15⅞" (40 x 40.3 cm.). The Museum of Modern Art, New York, gift of Kleiner, Bell and Co.

Among the many contributions made by Josef Albers to the art of printmaking were his efforts to create in silkscreen and lithography correct impressions of the interaction of colors. Until the 1960s Albers's prints had been executed in black or embossed without ink. Then, in 1962, he began to create the silkscreen prints for his great teaching opus, *The Interaction of Color*, with two colleagues in New Haven, Norman Ives and Sewell Sillman. In these systematic illustrations of his theories, Albers provided Ives and Sillman with geometrical drawings and color swatches, which they reproduced. Even in his painting series *Homage to the Square*, which encompasses some of these theories, Albers used unmixed paint directly from the tube, to guarantee the future possibility of reproducing the painting with identical materials. Nevertheless, Albers still painted by hand, and when he went to Tamarind Lithography Workshop in 1963–64 he worked directly with the lithographic materials. There, for the first time he used the transparency of ink as a means of deriving a change in color, and still he was able to achieve the potentiality of sensing visual phenomena such as color transpositions or auras occurring at the edges of the concentric squares. Flat, unmodulated color was the necessary ingredient for the active visual movement that Albers wished to induce. At a moment when color prints were finding an enthusiastic audience, Albers's work provided the laboratory experiments that would expand the potential of the medium. The brilliant colors of his lithographs and silkscreens, heralding those of the Op Artists and "hard edge" painters, awakened others to the serious study of the way color is experienced.

80. Ad Reinhardt. Plate from *10 Screenprints by Ad Reinhardt*. 1966. Published by Ives-Sillman, Inc. Silkscreen, 13³⁄₁₆ x 10" (33.5 x 25.4 cm.). The Museum of Modern Art, New York, John B. Turner Fund

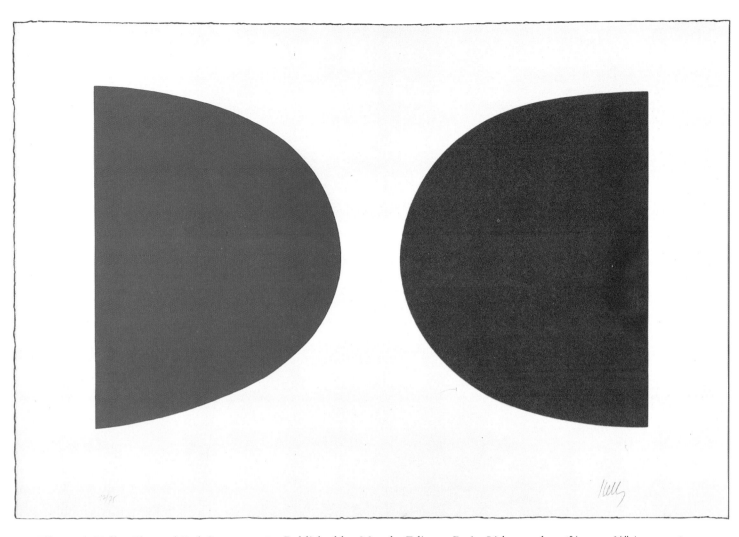

81. Ellsworth Kelly. *Blue and Red-Orange*. 1964. Published by Maeght Editeur, Paris. Lithograph, 16⁵⁄₁₆ x 27³⁄₈″ (41.4 x 69.5 cm.). The Museum of Modern Art, New York, given anonymously

82. Ellsworth Kelly. *Conques* from *Third Curve Series*. 1976. Published by Gemini G.E.L. Lithograph and debossing, 29 x 22″ (73.7 x 55.9 cm.). © copyright Gemini G.E.L., Los Angeles, California, 1976

83. Alexander Liberman. Untitled. 1961. Lithograph, 12⁵⁄₁₆ x 23¹³⁄₁₆″ (31.3 x 60.5 cm.). The Museum of Modern Art, New York, gift of the artist

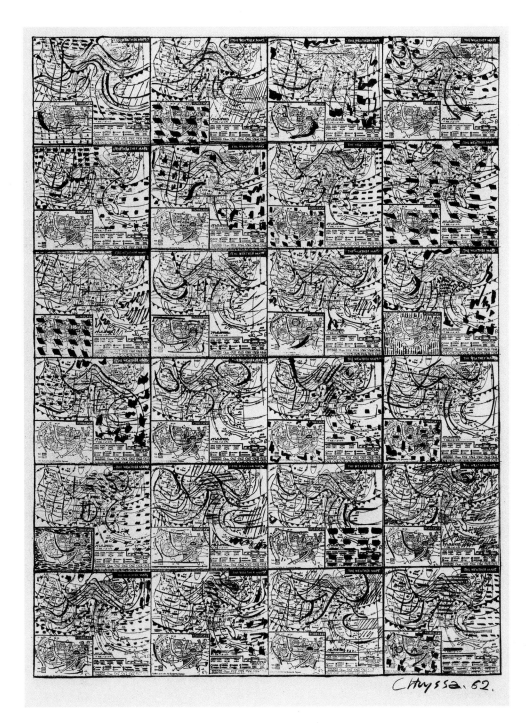

84. Chryssa. *Weather Map* from *Newspaper Book*. 1962.
Published by Leo Steinberg. Photo-lithograph on cloth,
29¹³⁄₁₆ x 21½" (75.7 x 54.6 cm.). The Museum of Modern
Art, New York, gift of the artist

The Greek-born sculptor Chryssa forms most of her works
out of letters. Since the late 1950s she has used both lead and
neon tubing to project the stylized symbols, without relating
them to language. Associated more with the European movement of Lettrisme (wherein masses of letters were handled
abstractly) than with artists such as Jasper Johns and Jim Dine
(who were enchanted with the ambiguity of the words they
placed in their compositions), Chryssa displayed her commitment to letters in ways which anticipated the concerns of
Structuralist and Minimalist artists. Repetitive forms, set out
in a regular pattern, became the formula for her sculpture and
later painting. Her neon sculpture, which captured the look
of Times Square advertising, was interpreted as a Pop manifestation, and the Kineticists claimed it for its dazzling optical
effects. As this example of her printmaking shows, as early as
1962 Chryssa was using formalized elements as the subject of
her art. The series of twenty-two prints of her *Newspaper
Book*, made on a Lithoprint press from actual pages of *The
New York Times*, still incorporates a good deal of expressionist
brushwork over some of the newsprint, relating it to the sort
of work Rauschenberg was creating at the time. However,
Chryssa's path led elsewhere, and her choice of the particularly rigid structure of this print is a forecast of the stricter
formalist art of the 1970s.

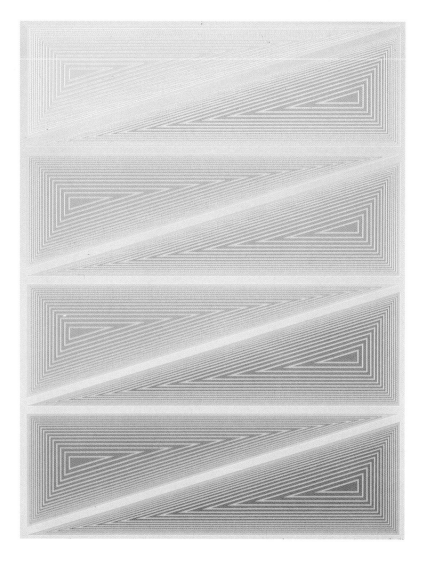

85. Richard Anuszkiewicz. Plate 6 from
The Inward Eye by William Blake. 1970.
Published by Aquarius Press, Baltimore.
Silkscreen, 25¾ x 19⅞″ (65.4 x 50.5 cm.)

86. Frank Stella. *Jasper's Dilemma.* 1973. Published
by Petersburg Press, Ltd. Offset lithograph,
8⅝ x 17¼″ (21.9 x 43.8 cm.)

87. Gene Davis. *Checkmate.* 1972. Published by Petersburg Press, Ltd. Lithograph, 24⅛ x 14½″ (61.3 x 36.8 cm.). The Museum of Modern Art, New York, John B. Turner Fund

The linear arrangement of color which dominated the work of many painters in the 1960s, including Morris Louis, Kenneth Noland, and the much younger Frank Stella, rarely found a comfortable place in printmaking. The precarious balances of color which formed the fundamental structure of such art could be reproduced by a silkscreen printer, but the vitality that jumped from the canvas was somehow lacking, absorbed by the dull sameness of the printed surface. Among the few prints that have successfully conveyed the subtle nature of the strictly constructed color imagery of so-called post-painterly abstraction is this lithograph by Gene Davis. With extremely fine lines of different hues, Davis has presented an agreeable distribution of emphasis, warmer and brighter colors passing between cooler and less sharply visible tones. Similar to a colored pencil drawing, this print lacks the impact that might be expected from the heavy impression of a lithographic stone, but the color does not lie on the surface, as pencil does; it appears engulfed in the soft gray handmade paper.

88. Ed Moses. *Broken Wedge* 5. 1973. Published by
Cirrus Editions. Lithograph, 24 x 18″ (61.0 x
45.7 cm.)

89. Jules Olitski. Untitled. 1968. Lithograph, 29⅞ x 21¼″
(75.8 x 54.0 cm.). The Museum of Modern Art, New York, gift
of Mrs. Sadye M. Lee

90. OPPOSITE Kenneth Noland. *Horizontal Stripes* (III–9). 1978.
Produced and published by Tyler Graphics Ltd. Artist-made paper, hand-painted, 51 x 32″ (129.5 x 81.3 cm.). © copyright Kenneth Noland/Tyler Graphics Ltd. 1978

91. Robert Ryman. Plate from *Six Aquatints*. 1975. Published by Parasol Press Ltd. Aquatint, 35¼ x 35½″ (89.5 x 90.2 cm.)

92. Robert Mangold. Plate from *Seven Aquatints*. 1973. Published by Parasol Press Ltd. Aquatint, 15⅞ x 15¾″ (40.3 x 40.0 cm.)

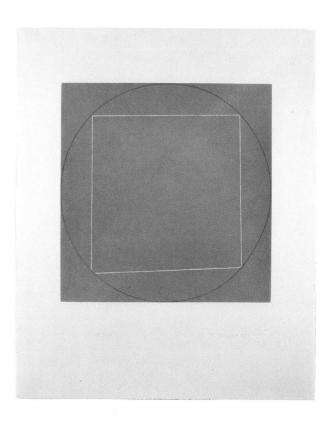

93. Brice Marden. Plate from *Five Plates*. 1973. Published by Parasol Press Ltd. Etching and aquatint, 27⅝ x 19⅞″ (70.2 x 50.0 cm.)

94. Barnett Newman. Untitled II. 1969. Published by Universal Limited Art Editions. Etching and aquatint, 23⅜ x 14¹³⁄₁₆″ (59.4 x 37.6 cm.)

95. Fred Sandback. Untitled. 1975. Published by Heiner Friedrich, Munich. Etching, 11¹¹⁄₁₆ x 15¹⁵⁄₁₆″ (29.7 x 40.5 cm.)

Possibly the most extreme example of Minimalist print-making is the work of Fred Sandback. Hypersensitive to materials and their determination of spatial factors, he has pared down the number of elements and his manipulation of them to the barest minimum. In this etching these elements consist of a rectangular copperplate upon which the artist scored five lines, a rectangular piece of silky Japanese paper slightly tan in tone, and the printing of the plate, horizontally placed on the paper, in black ink. While all this seems childishly simple, its radical simplicity provokes increased attention to the minute effects that are produced. Among the subtle physical properties given form by the few steps outlined above are the changes in dimension caused by the impression of the plate into soft paper, and the pale shadow of ink left on the plate that occupies the flattened surface of the paper and affects the perception of space surrounding the now jutting vertical black line. This nearly three-dimensional composition presents spatial effects similar to Sandback's environmental works of the same period. In such pieces, the artist segments a room by affixing taut string or yarn to ceiling and floor, creating an illusion of large, transparent planes intersecting the open space.

96. Dorothea Rockburne. Plate from *Locus Series*. 1972–75. Published by Parasol Press Ltd. Aquatint and relief etching, 39⅞ x 30″ (101.3 x 76.2 cm.)

129/150   S Lewitt

97. Sol LeWitt. Plate 5 from *Composite Series*. 1970. Published by Sarah Lawrence Press. Silkscreen, 20 x 20"
(50.8 x 50.8 cm.). The Museum of Modern Art, New York

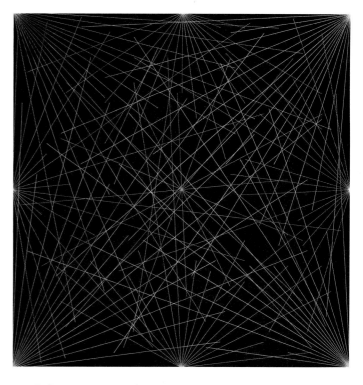

98. Sol LeWitt. *Lines from Sides, Corners and Center*. 1977.
Published by Parasol Press Ltd. Etching and aquatint, 34⅝ x
34⅞" (87.9 x 88.6 cm.)

    The basis of a set of monumental wall drawings and a series
of silkscreens, the configuration of this print follows a pattern
established by the artist in drawings and prints in the early
1970s. Many of LeWitt's earliest drawings (for sculpture,
walls, and prints) were based upon quite simple instructions:
lines—horizontal, vertical, and diagonal—executed in black
and/or the primary colors (red, yellow, and blue). All the lines
in these compositions began and ended at the edges of rectangular or square shapes. When LeWitt began to work away
from the edges, diagonal lines of finite lengths required more
detailed instructions for their exact placement. These instructions accompanied each drawn line in two series of etchings LeWitt made at Crown Point Press, the handwritten
sentences decorating the side of each carefully placed, exact-
length line. While it was fascinating to have both the instructions and the consequent composition in one work, LeWitt's
terse mode of art-making was best evolved without so much
verbiage. This aquatint, printed in white over a lightly grid-
ded black ground, illustrates how the surface of a particular
medium can control the entire sense of the work. By creating
a velvety, light-absorbing background, the artist has provided
an infinite space upon which seemingly random lines radiate
in all directions. The slightly visible pattern of the grid controls these lines, preventing them from entering the void of
the black aquatint ground.

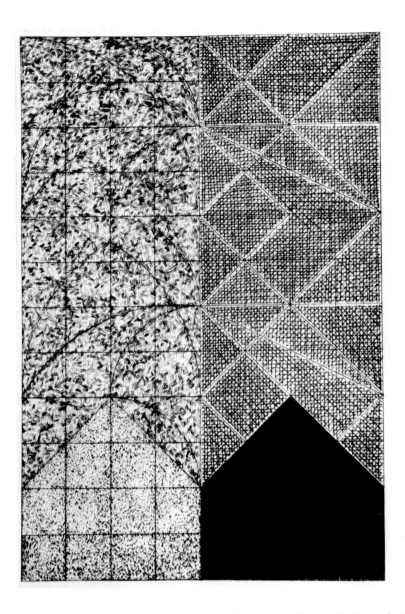

99. Jennifer Bartlett. *Day and Night*, from a series of three. 1978. Published by Multiples, Inc. Drypoint, 30¾ x 20¾" (78.1 x 52.7 cm.). Brooke Alexander, Inc.

Among the artists who found regular, modular formats the ultimate expression of formalist art, Jennifer Bartlett made unique use of the grid. Manufacturing squares covered with a grid pattern, she created compositions of dozens of these squares, each embellished with colored dots within their linear networks. Placed together, the dots formed recognizable objects, sometimes of Pop subjects, and the variety of images became distinct only as distance melded the dots together. In this, one of her first prints, Bartlett fills in the spaces of one side of the grid with curved drypoint stabs, the other side with straight lines, finally covering the total surface and revealing some of the spirit of the title. In the other two versions of this composition, enriched with both line and color (printed in yellows and reds in one, blues and browns in the other), the sum of the additions offers interesting variations on the theme. Such variations are a particular aspect of Bartlett's work, as basic to it as the modular construct. In the most ambitious of her early prints, *Graceland Mansion* (1979), Bartlett created five works, each in a different medium and each composed of a slightly different view of the building. In two of the prints, the image was revealed by the pattern of marks no longer constricted by a grid, indicating the freer manner she has pursued since that time.

100. Donald Judd. *6-L*. 1961–69. Woodcut, 25⅝ x 15¹⁵⁄₁₆″ (65.1 x 40.5 cm.). The Museum of Modern Art, New York, gift of Philip Johnson

101. Michael Heizer. *Scrap Metal Drypoint #2*. 1978. Published by Gemini G.E.L. Drypoint, 29⅛ x 79⅞″ (74.0 x 191.7 cm.). © copyright Gemini G.E.L. Los Angeles, California, 1978

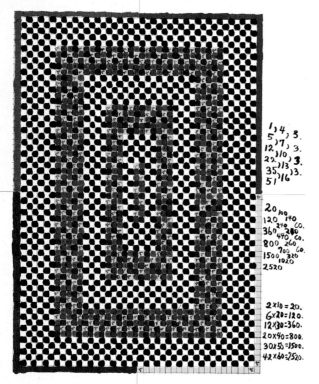

$1, 4, 3.$
$5) 7, 3.$
$12) 10, 3.$
$22) 13, 3.$
$35) 13) 3.$
$51) 16) 3.$

$20, 100$
$120, 140$
$360, 240, 60.$
$440, 60.$
$800, 260$
$700, 60.$
$1500, 320$
1020
2520

$2 \times 10 = 20.$
$6 \times 20 = 120.$
$12 \times 30 = 360.$
$20 \times 40 = 800.$
$30 \times 50 = 1500.$
$42 \times 60 = 2520.$

$7 \times 360 = 2520.$

102. Alfred Jensen. Plate from *A Pythagorean Notebook*. 1965. Lithograph, $22\frac{5}{8}$ x $16\frac{1}{2}$" (57.4 x 41.9 cm.). The Museum of Modern Art, New York, gift of Kleiner Bell & Co.

103. OPPOSITE Agnes Denes. *Dialectic Triangulation: A Visual Philosophy*. 1970. Esthetograph (monotype), 40 x 32" (101.6 x 81.3 cm.). © 1970 the artist

A strong intellectual current in creative expression at the end of the 1960s produced many unfamiliar and unexpected forms of art. Where so-called idea art actually became imagery, its compositional elements often came from technical graphic sources. When Agnes Denes began her exploration of the constructs that were used to explain theory, she adapted the tables, graphs, and symbols that are usually found in textbooks and other conveyors of visual information. Basing her own graphic images on such analytical charts, she has produced schematic imagery that, like this print, examines a chosen subject with intensive thoroughness. In 1969 Denes worked on the subject of dialectic triangulation, producing in 1970 a print of a mechanical drawing in which she investigated, through diagrammatic forms, the idea of triangulation. As she writes in the body of the print, "Dialectic Triangulation is an art definition. It refers to a process leading to the visualization of mechanisms and hypotheses. It is the application of inquiries to aspects of human existence and knowledge." She continues, "This type of art is analytical; it goes beyond illusionism and deals with realities." The means of producing the print is equally a part of the artist's attitude toward process: she has named her medium "esthetograph," even though technically it is no different from the photographic printing mediums, such as blueprint and Ozalid, that are commonly used for architectural and engineering plans.

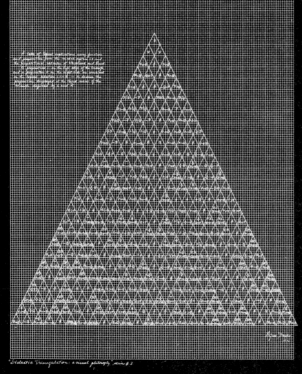

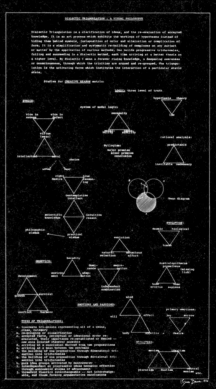

104. John Cage. *Not Wanting to Say Anything About Marcel.* 1969. Published by Eye Editions. Color lithograph, 26½ x 38⅝" (67.3 x 98.1 cm.). Carl Solway Gallery, Cincinnati, Ohio

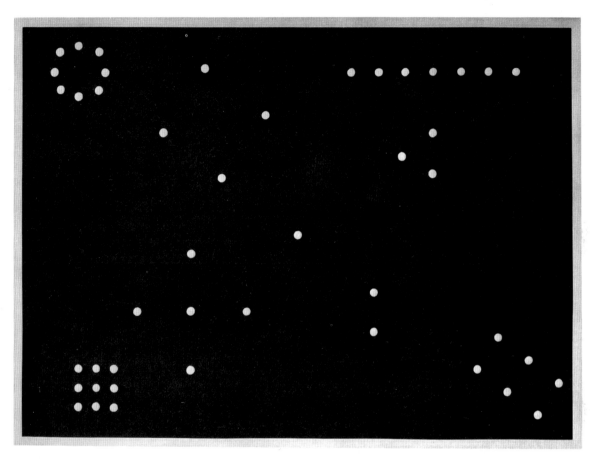

105. Mel Bochner. *Rules of Inference*. 1974. Published by Parasol Press Ltd. Aquatint, 22¼ x 31 ¹⁄₁₆″ (56.5 x 78.9 cm.)

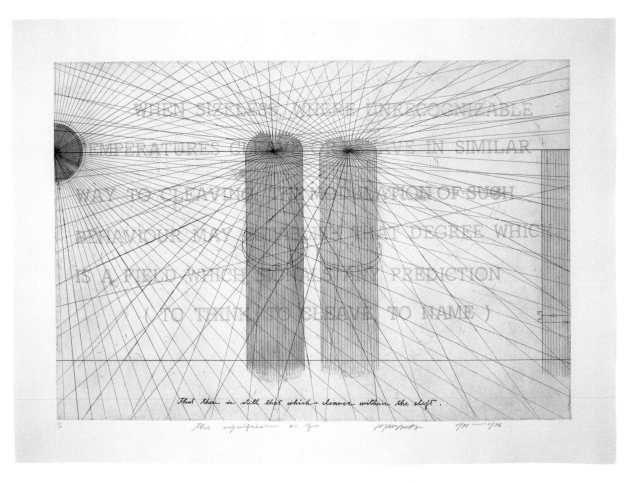

106. Shusaku Arakawa. *The signified or if (No. 2)*. 1975–76. Published by Multiples, Inc. Etching and aquatint, 23¹³⁄₁₆ x 35½″ (60.5 x 90.2 cm.)

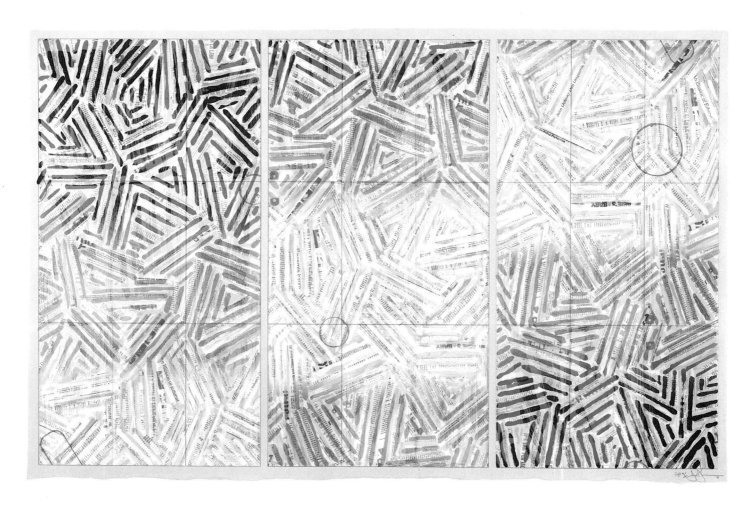

107. Jasper Johns. *Usuyuki*. 1980. Silkscreen, 28¾ x 45⅜″ (73.0 x 115.2 cm.). Co-published by the artist and Simca Print Artists, Inc. © Jasper Johns. Courtesy Simca Print Artists, Inc.

108. Richard Estes. Plate from *Urban Landscapes 3*. 1981.
Published by Parasol Press Ltd. Silkscreen, 14 x 20″
(35.6 x 50.8 cm.)

109. Alex Katz. *Red Coat*. 1983 Co-published by the artist
and Simca Print Artists, Inc. Silkscreen, 58 x 29″
(147.3 x 73.7 cm.)

110. Chuck Close. *Keith*. 1972. Published by Parasol Press Ltd. Mezzotint, 45⅝ x 35½″ (116.0 x 90.0 cm.).
The Museum of Modern Art, New York,
John B. Turner Fund

The Photorealist painter Chuck Close chose one of the most time-consuming, if not most difficult, techniques to create his first mature print. Encouraged by the publisher Robert Feldman to make a print using his formula of building compositions from one-inch squares derived from a grid superimposed over his photographic portraits, Close went to the Oakland, California, workshop of Kathan Brown, an expert intaglio printmaker. Attempting to prepare the nearly four-foot plate for the artist, Brown found it impossible to cover so large a surface evenly with the texture produced by a hand rocker. Brown decided to photo-etch the texture, which produced an overall surface of pits which the artist could burnish in order to evolve his image. As Close had never worked in this manner, proofs were printed after each square was completed, so that in the finished prints the area of the mouth where he first worked is much lighter because the pits had become nearly flattened and no longer retained as much ink as elsewhere. Even though this unevenness dispersed somewhat the impact of the shallow, photographic field of focus, the print is an impressive example of the formalist device applied to a realistic image. By imposing a grid as the structure upon which the image is formed, Close retains the essence of formalism—the picture as reality as opposed to reality being pictured.

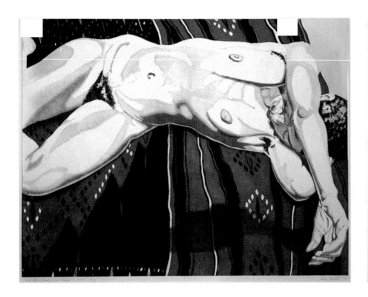

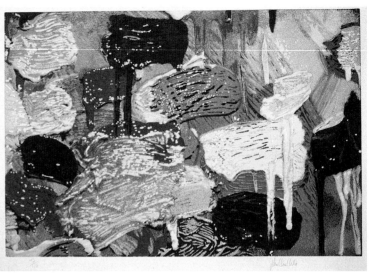

111. Philip Pearlstein. *Nude Lying on Black and Red Blanket.* 1974. Aquatint and etching, 22¼ x 29¼″ (56.2 x 74.3 cm.). © Philip Pearlstein. Courtesy Frumkin Gallery

112. John Clem Clarke. *Color Abstract.* 1972. Published by Brooke Alexander, Inc. Silkscreen, 23⅞ x 36″ (60.7 x 91.5 cm.)

113. Louise Nevelson. Untitled. 1967. Color lithograph, diptych, each sheet 39⅜ x 27⅝″ (100.0 x 70.2 cm.). Courtesy Pace Gallery

114. Joyce Kozloff. *Longing.* 1977. Collage of lithographs *(Pictures and Borders),* with colored pencil, 92 x 41″ (233.7 x 104.1 cm.). Courtesy Mintz, Levin, Cohn, Ferris, Glovsky and Popeo, P. C.

115. Robert Morris. *Steam* from the portfolio *Earth Projects*. 1969. Color lithograph, 20 x 27¹⁵⁄₁₆″ (50.8 x 71.0 cm.)

117. OPPOSITE Richard Artschwager. *Interior (Woodgrain) #2.* 1977. Published by Multiples, Inc. Drypoint, 9¹⁵⁄₁₆ x 11⁵⁄₁₆″ (25.2 x 28.7 cm.). Brooke Alexander, Inc.

Richard Artschwager worked for a decade in a furniture factory, and it is not surprising that he turned to the materials with which he was familiar when he devised his unique sculpture in the early 1960s. He used patterned Formica, that impenetrable flat veneer that hides flaws, for geometric sculptures that most often took the forms of tables and chairs. While Artschwager's work of the 1960s was stylistically akin to Pop Art, his subsequent production, including a Formica-covered box containing lozenge-shaped objects made of a variety of materials from glass to upholstery hair, indicated more concern with ideas such as deception and distortion than with the new reality. This small drypoint print shows an arrangement of objects in an interior, their forms dominated by the pattern of woodgrain of which they are made (or with which they are masked). The print's title divulges the intention of the artist, since "woodgrain" indicates that he has created a variation on the theme of "interior." Several other prints are closely related to Artschwager's paintings of buildings, landscapes, and interiors on surfaces of regularly patterned, commercial, texturized material that consists of whorls in slight relief, mimicking a stucco wall finish. Besides the distortion arising from the underlying pattern, the objects in the compositions are presented in a manner that confuses ordinary expectations. In Artschwager's largest print, a silkscreen also done in 1977, an interior is shown from two very slightly different viewpoints, side by side. Even in this drypoint the acute perspective makes the bowl in the foreground gigantic and tricks us into perceiving the camouflaged carpet as the surface upon which it stands.

116. Christo. *Wrapped Whitney* from the portfolio *(Some) Not Realized Projects.* 1971. Published by Landfall Press, Inc. Color lithograph and collage, 27⅞ x 21⅞" (70.8 x 55.5 cm.). Brooke Alexander, Inc.

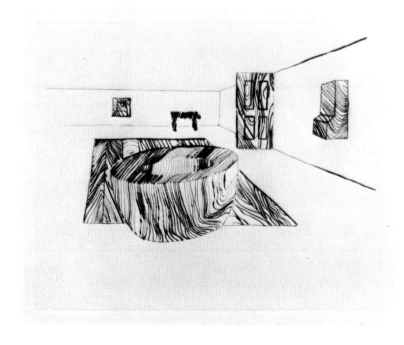

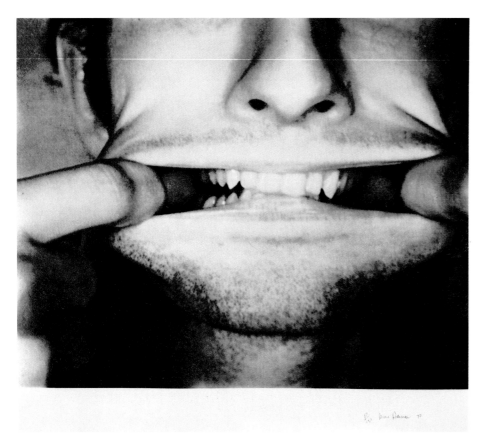

118. Bruce Nauman. Plate from *Studies for Holograms*. 1970. Published by
Aetna Studios. Silkscreen, 20⅜ x 26″ (51.7 x 66.0 cm.)

119. Les Levine. Plate from *Iris Print-out Portrait*. 1969. Silkscreen, 7⁹⁄₁₆ x 24⅞″ (43.7 x 63.2 cm.)

120. Otto Piene. Plate from the portfolio *Sky Art*. 1969. Color lithograph, 35⅛ x 25⅛″ (89.2 x 63.8 cm.). The Museum of Modern Art, New York, gift of Kleiner, Bell and Co.

121. Vito Acconci. *Stones for a Wall No. 7.* 1977. Published by Landfall Press, Inc. Color lithograph, 30³⁄₁₆ x 23³⁄₄″ (76.7 x 60.3 cm.). © Landfall Press, Inc., Chicago, Illinois

CHAPTER FIVE

With the exception of Photorealism, the tradition of depicting recognizable objects weakened considerably during the 1970s. Only a few artists seemed concerned to give what was shown in their works as much or more significance as the manner in which it was organized, but these few felt it to be necessary to affect the viewer directly, touch an emotion or establish a rapport through a familiar and comfortable subject. Where the meaning of a picture derives from something more than the process by which it has been made or its own physical proportions and material, then an entire range of expression is possible.

Robert Rauschenberg continued to make many prints that celebrated or commemorated real events. His series of thirty-three lithographs *Stoned Moon*, done after he had been invited by the National Aeronautics and Space Administration to witness the successful launching of Apollo II, was filled with homey, familiar Florida subjects (palm trees, oranges, and such) and photographic images of the rockets and astronauts (Fig. 52). *Sky Garden* (1969) was the central print in the series and was, appropriately, larger vertically than any print published anywhere up to that time. While remaining succinctly a Rauschenberg image, the instantly identifiable subject gave the viewer an unavoidable personal relationship with the abstract composition (Fig. 122). Throughout the 1970s Rauschenberg's prints continued to refer to topical or historical events. He also made five editions of clay pieces at Graphicstudio at the University of South Florida at Tampa in 1973 and, in the same year, was the first prominent artist actually to devise works in handmade paper (Fig. 123), which he did at Ambert, France.

Artists' desire to work with wet, unformed paper pulp was, perhaps, a sign that latent primordial tendencies were beginning to emerge. Concurrent with their cerebral investigations of art-making processes were more intuitive, hands-on explorations of crafts that could be used to express personal and emotional themes. In the early 1970s, Alan Shields was among the first to print patterns on paper that was cut into strips and woven like cloth. Working with William Weege in Wisconsin, Shields increasingly used craft techniques (including handmade paper) and dime-store materials (such as glitter and glue) to make his abstract but patently ritualistic prints. Shields's work has a superficial relationship to the pattern art that had some legitimacy within the context of process art. However, from its spiritual genesis, more or less reflecting the interests of the disenchanted youth of the late 1960s, grew a progressively stronger tendency to move away from mechanical, predictable, and technically pristine printmaking into more primitive, spontaneous forms such as paperworks and monotypes (Fig. 124).

Whereas handicrafts had normally been associated with individual home-work, the aspirations of artists who wished to make multiple works in less perfectible materials required craftsmen whom, in more contemporary terms, we know as technicians. Garner Tullis was one of the first to make artworks solely from hand-made paper. He opened his California workshop in 1973, and made it possible for Louise Nevelson, Sam Francis, Kenneth Noland, and several other well-established artists to combine printing or embossing with papermaking. In 1973 Ken Tyler encouraged Rauschenberg to work with paper, going with him to the French mill that made paper for Gemini's lithographic editions. A year and a half later the artist went to India under the auspices of Gemini, and at the Gandhi Ashram made paper out of local materials (spices, mud, and cloth). Only a few months earlier, Rauschenberg, who had consistently used textiles in his assemblages, created a series of unique and edition works entitled *Hoarfrosts*, which consisted of freely floating veils of cloth, printed with photographic images. His work has its origins in emotion rather than intellect, and thus provides one legitimate link between Abstract Expressionism and the several identities that are lumped together as Neo-Expressionism.

Frank Stella's art underwent a significant transformation after he subjected his formal compositions to the inconsistencies of hand-molded paper and undertook the arduous labor of hand-coloring 138 paper reliefs. Another project initiated by Ken Tyler after he opened his own studio, Stella's series *Paper Reliefs* (1975, Fig. 125), was the first of several collaborations with the printer which eventually included the fabrication of mammoth, unique constructions of French curves made of honeycomb-core materials originally developed for airplanes.

The radical changes in Stella's work reflected an alteration in sensitivity which, after the brilliantly colored but blatantly mechanical "protractor" paintings, manifested itself in a freer, more plastic rendition of geometric forms. His decision to use shapes derived from the draftsman's French curve automatically engendered a greater sense of depth and movement than had been possible in the less complex constructs he had used previously. It was possible to see in these works relationships with the graffiti that had been spray-painted over walls and subway cars by New

York City youths. The careening shapes of eccentrically designed letters, baldly encroaching upon each other with clashing colors and frenzied interior scribbles, were a form of contemporary folk art that had many layers of social meaning. While Stella's works in this vein were not meant to be subjective statements about the environment in which graffiti made its militant statement, their reference to the formal elements of street art changed our perception. The first lithographs and silkscreens that derived from the constructions based on French curves lacked their sense of movement and depth, as Stella attempted to brush and draw the areas that, when printed, gave little idea of the flair and daring instability of the painted surfaces. Nonetheless, Stella put more and more effort into printmaking, both with Tyler (*Exotic Birds* of 1977 was the first series using French curves) and with prints that he made for Petersburg Press at the offset press in his home (*Shards*, 1982). He finally achieved a way of making works of handmade paper, metal, and wood engraving that were intrinsically printed statements rather than translations of earlier, unique compositions (Fig. 126). Making nearly all of his graphic works in close collaboration with printers, Stella appears to be the ultimate product of the print workshop's domination of the 1960s and '70s.

Other artists whose prints are colorful yet mysterious evocations of the pervasive urban vernacular are Sam Gilliam and Nancy Graves. Gilliam, a Washingtonian whose work contains obvious elements of Lyric Abstraction, made draped painted cloth environments in the early 1970s. His lithographic prints of textured and crumpled paper, stained with layers of colors, are, similarly, records of his past experiences (Fig. 127). Graves first came to public attention with a sculptured group of stuffed, life-size camels. While her earliest prints were based on more or less romanticized lunar maps, later etchings of brightly colored jottings show a sensitivity to the irrational and unpredictable aspects of human activity (Fig. 128).

Before discussing the works of younger figurative artists who came to prominence during the latter years of the 1970s, we should mention a few older artists who had special ideas about figuration but were not central participants in any one of the movements previously discussed. Both Richard Lindner and Romare Bearden created imagery that was extremely illustrative of their personal views of contemporary society. Lindner was associated at times with Pop Art, but his work had its roots in the Neue Sachlichkeit (New Objectivity) of post–World War I Germany. He translated his viciously satirical watercolors into lithographs, most notably the series titled *Fun City* (1971, Fig. 129). Like many European artists (he came to America from Germany in 1941), he was satisfied with the *chromiste*'s renditions of his work and took little time to perfect his images during the printing process. Romare Bearden's work consists of collages of magazine photographs transformed by his editing scissors into poetic views of the black community. Using a technique appropriate to a portrayal of those who have little means except the refuse of an affluent society which, in turn, evokes their poverty, Bearden paints over and around the cut-out shapes and images. Although he has made few prints, those few are a sensitive statement in serious artistic form about a primary issue of our time (Fig. 130).

Red Grooms is another artist who has found contemporary life full of material for his cartoon-like commentary. Not only has he made gigantic constructions of entire areas of the New York landscape (*Ruckus Manhattan*, 1975), in which he humorously portrays the infinite variety of its inhabitants, but he has directed his friendly satire at the art world as well. Like many of his contemporaries, Grooms quotes other artists or refers to personalities in the world of art with the confidence that their familiarity will enhance our appreciation. Since 1958 he has made numerous prints that energetically conjure up the confusion of city life, and he has appropriated the paper-doll cut-out as a means of emphasizing the playfulness and wit of his images. His cut-out lithograph *Gertrude* (1975, Fig. 133), a portrait of Gertrude Stein, the famous writer and collector of paintings by Picasso, Matisse, and others, was a homespun parody of Picasso's celebrated portrait.

Such quotations abound in the 1970s and early 1980s: Roy Lichtenstein's painted and printed derivations of Surrealist and German Expressionist works (the latter particularly timely as both American and German artists returned to those sources for inspiration); David Hockney's appropriation of Matisse's fluid black line in his black and white lithographs and his compositional and coloristic references to the prints of Edvard Munch in other lithographs; and Jasper Johns's oblique citation of Munch's self-portrait in his series of lithographs and monotypes of the familiar Savarin can filled with brushes, now with the skeletal arm extracted from Munch's composition and placed below the main image (Fig. 136). In almost all of these works one can detect the underlying, rather arch humor of the cognoscenti.

The masters of such quotations have been the artists who developed within Pop Art. It was inevitable that some of them would use their trademark styles in works that contradicted their earlier iconoclastic intentions. The sublimely poetic aquatints of Claes Oldenburg, for example, still represent outsize, strangely sited objects, but where earlier works would mimic the pretension of traditional establishments and aesthetic formalities, the grand *Screwarch Bridge* (1980) is a homage, in spirit and manner, to Charles Meryon, the slightly morbid nineteenth-century Parisian etcher of views along the Seine (Fig. 137).

The many recent exhibitions devoted to late nineteenth-century and early twentieth-century artists and movements could not fail to have repercussions upon the careers of even younger artists who studied art history in school and pored over the art magazines. Robert Kushner took many of the primitive borrowings of the German Expressionists for his repetitive compositions of tribal dancers and other rhythmic subjects. His prints are occasionally printed on "fancy" decorative papers, the patterns of which act as a web or network joining colorful, outlined shapes. Unlike the type of pattern art that arose out of more diligent considerations of process, Kushner's figurative compositions, while repetitive, are suffused with a compelling inner spirit, which lends them an illusory decorative quality (Fig. 138).

It is, perhaps, the return of mystery as a motivating element that altered the face of art in the late 1970s. For example, the work of Jim Dine, formerly presented with little affectation although always extremely personal, became enveloped in a haze of lines, smudges, and atmospheric shading. By 1977 his well-known bathrobe had been transformed into a totemic, often ominous, object (Fig. 139). New subjects, such as gnarled trees and portraits of himself and his wife, Nancy, are imbued with drama and a sense of uncertainty.

Accompanying this emphasis upon the subjective was a patent lack of interest in uniformity and a nearly subversive intent to sabotage the equilibrium of the print establishment. During the late 1970s, the Metropolitan Museum of Art in New York announced an exhibition, "The Painterly Print" (shown in 1980), which it meant to be a historical review of one form of printmaking, the monotype. Jim Dine had first tried in 1975 to combine an etched self-portrait with colors applied to the plate for each run. Even earlier Helen Frankenthaler had added monotype passages to lithographs, but neither she nor Dine intended to make a totally monotype composition. In 1973–74 Adolph Gottlieb, inhibited by a paralyzing stroke, made use of the etching press in his studio and, like the ailing Milton Avery in 1954, produced many monotypes. As the monotypes of Degas were published and his technique became more widely understood, it was inevitable that the painters who had access to the incomparable equipment of a print workshop would try, in much larger formats than Degas had used, their hand at this form. Michael Mazur, a figurative artist of the 1960s, was the most serious in this attempt, recognizing a characteristic of the process that he could exploit: that he could take another print from his painted plate by enhancing the remains of ink left from the first printing, either by merely adding more color or by adding new figures (Fig. 140). The luminosity of printing inks or oil paints and their "marriage" with the paper, obtainable only in the printing process, characterize this essentially painterly procedure. Helpful as it is to have assistance in printing monotypes, it is really a solitary occupation, and only in the works of Mazur and others who exploit the extension of the residue of the first printing is there much graphic expression involved.

Less attention to precision in graphic techniques coincided with changes in the work of some well-established artists and a revival of interest in some who were long out of step with the directions art had taken since the late 1950s. About fifteen years before his death in 1980, the Abstract Expressionist painter Philip Guston began to add figurative references to his forms. Although he had made a few abstract prints at the Tamarind and Hollander workshops in 1963 and 1966, like many of his stylistic colleagues he had little proclivity for printmaking. Only in the last year of his life did he produce a series of black and white lithographs at Gemini that incorporate his evolved figurative style. The massive shapes that form themselves into chairs, cigarette butts, and heaps of cast-off shoes contain vague echoes of Oldenburg's early drawings and some of Grooms's humor, but are pervaded with both mystery and cynicism. The spirit that motivated and magnified his abstract painting is compressed into Guston's created world of discards. Not identifiably an expression of protest, Guston's late work must nevertheless be seen in the context of a world constantly abraded by reactions to injustice, affirmations of one philosophy to the exclusion of all others, and the terror of man's own inventions (Fig. 142).

Leon Golub might stand for all those artists who never stopped depicting man in this no-win situation. His emotional portrayal of "everyman" struck a responsive chord once again in the late 1970s as the appeal of intellectualized formalism wore thin. However, the return to a more expressive art did not signal its rebirth as a means of active protest, but rather its usefulness as a distrustful representation of our dilemma. Most of Golub's emotional content is in the rendering of line, choice of medium, harsh color, intentionally badly constructed figures and compositions, and editing. A moment in the course of an event, the fleeting glance at a scene or an object, are part of the artist's means of describing the nightmare of real life (Fig. 143).

Unlike the Surrealists, who dredged up from the subconscious all sorts of anxieties and pleasures, the figurative artists of the 1980s look to a less purposefully induced interpretation of the mysterious unknown. Several hark back to the "primitive" tendencies that permeated many of the early works of those Abstract Expressionists who found an infinite source of potent imagery in Indian pictographs and other magical representations. There seems to be, however, a tendency to emulate rather than portray the motifs of spiritual or magical ritual. Susan Rothenberg has painted horses in a manner that represents them as archaic, sacred spirits. Her prints, particularly the woodcuts, enlarge upon the inherently ritualistic procedure of the creation of such art. While it is unlikely that incantations accompany the cutting of her blocks or the scraping of her stones, the images that emerge have the quality of magically formed drawings in dimly lit caves (Fig. 144).

Two artists who have worked predominantly in woodcut have chosen to portray disastrous occurrences as a means of articulating the mysterious mission of the art experience. Richard Bosman, the son of a peripatetic sea captain, makes anxiety-laden paintings and prints that capture moments of tragedy or fear, frozen in mid-action, like a single frame of a cartoon strip. But unlike Lichtenstein's "cartoons," Bosman's compositions are rough, imperfect, and nearly inarticulate renditions of events (Fig. 145). The use of woodcut in Louisa Chase's similarly dramatic prints enhances their ominous character (Fig. 146). Oddly, the spiritual tradition of trees as containers of important secrets continues to permeate woodcuts conceived with underlying emotional content. Bosman and Chase do not arduously chisel their images into the wood in the privacy of their studios; rather, they go to the printer's shop where they use electric drills to cut the lines quickly, leaving larger areas for the printer to clear out methodically. Even though Chase has issued her prints in hand-colored as well as black and white editions, this is no longer a home-craft that the artist alone controls. The look of spontaneity that was so obviously a part of early German Expressionist art did not, it now seems, derive from an impetus that could take place only privately.

One similarity shared by the German Expressionists and later twentieth-century artists is that group activity is an important form of expression for both. Like the young architectural students of Die Brücke, some artists of our day have banded together to hold their own exhibitions in unexpected sites, presenting a sort of "people's art." Mirroring the New Wave and Punk factions of popular music, groups such as COLAB, Inc., have created an art as transitory as the latest pop hit. Inevitably, as an artist is identified and given some individual recognition, the ephemeral quality of his or her art is displaced by the demands of the marketplace. One of the curiosities of this situation is how quickly such blatantly anti-establishment work is accepted and promoted in the world of which it is most critical.

The immense marketing structure that arose during the period covered by this book has contributed to both the flourishing of art and the dilution of its power. Two artists who came to prominence around 1980 represent consummate examples of how talent can be combined with astute comprehension of current interests to produce art that is exceptional enough to be successfully promoted. Julian Schnabel and David Salle paint in the Neo-Expressionist vein, borrowing imagery from diverse sources, from Goya, Kokoschka, and Disney, to create imposingly novel (but not *too* novel) works. Salle's paintings are those of the prodigious art student whose technique is unquestionably at a high level, but whose cultural interests are colored by period nostalgia (in this case, the popular art of the 1950s), and whose subjects are often composed with graffiti-like abandon. Schnabel, in his early works, typically covered his canvases with broken plates or antlers to create chaotic surfaces for his selection of borrowed motifs. Both artists were asked to make prints soon after they achieved commercial success; both have created etchings that succinctly represent their facility to produce compositions that are as agreeably eclectic as their paintings (Figs. 149, 150). Salle has superimposed nudes over renderings of cartoon illustrations to produce a cacophony of styles and subjects. Schnabel depicts figures borrowed from other artists, spatters them with symbols, and defaces them with spastic lines. His prints are ambitious and massive, and summarize most of the factors that have contributed to the evolution of the print during the twentieth century.

Besides the expansion of scale and proficiency in the use of many mediums, printmaking has shared in nearly all the developments of art during the decades discussed in this book. Its audience has a more highly sophisticated visual memory than any previous culture possessed, so that images are instantly recognizable, although insight into meaning may have been diminished. Having become sensitized to the facture of art, we expect each physical element on the canvas or paper to stimulate some response or contribute to our understanding of the totality. The newer figurative art makes use of these responses and physical expectations, often in ways that seem suspiciously facile. The commercialism of fine art is traditionally suspect, particularly when figuration returns after a long period of abstraction. In this situation some thought might be given to similarities with the exhaustion of Paris as the world's art capital. Bernard Buffet represented the quintessence of the art dealer's dream, and his synthesis of the many factors that gave instant authority to his art led to his skyrocketing success. Subsequently, contemporary French art suffered a crisis of confidence. The fresh air then emanated from America. Now, as developments become ever more frantic after several decades of American dominance, the new breeze is coming from Europe.

Up until about 1980 little was known in America of the increasingly strong work of contemporary Germans and Italians, although some of the artists had visited New York or even spent time working there. These Europeans developed in the face of a nearly total commitment to American art by local galleries and collectors of contemporary work. Repeating the American experience of previous decades, they learned that confrontation with foreign art held in high esteem to the exclusion of almost everything done in one's own country creates intense competition.

Although there had been a continuous flow of foreign printmakers visiting and working at Pratt, and a few European painters had been given opportunities to make prints at Tamarind during the 1960s, only artists who chose to live in America for long periods of time were able to practice in the large workshops. One of the first Italians of this generation to gain international recognition, Francesco Clemente, went to Crown Point shortly after his first exhibition in New York and subsequently produced more than a dozen prints there (Fig. 151). Others (Enzo Cucchi, Sandro Chia, Mimmo Paladino) have either made prints in America or had their prints published by Americans.

The convenience of concluding a history on the same theme as it began, the encroachment of European art and artists on American culture, may seem too contrived. It appears, however, to be a fact; but the cliché of history repeating itself is not perfectly applicable. Rather than mature, gifted painters making an impact upon an impressionable, talented, but basically provincial community, as was the case in the 1940s, the influx of European artists in the 1980s arrives at the art capital of the world. As long as artists continue to create works that have physical form, all the communication facilities in the world will not replace the need for a marketplace. New York became that during the period this book covers, and its primacy as a showplace for all art in all forms stimulates further production of art and further encouragement of artists.

Because of the universal networks that now allow both the dispersal of information and the transport of people, the age-old function of the artist to communicate at a level beyond the expected and ordinary becomes something that touches more and more lives. When art can be transmitted and reconstituted in physical form through electronics, it will be printed art that circles the globe.

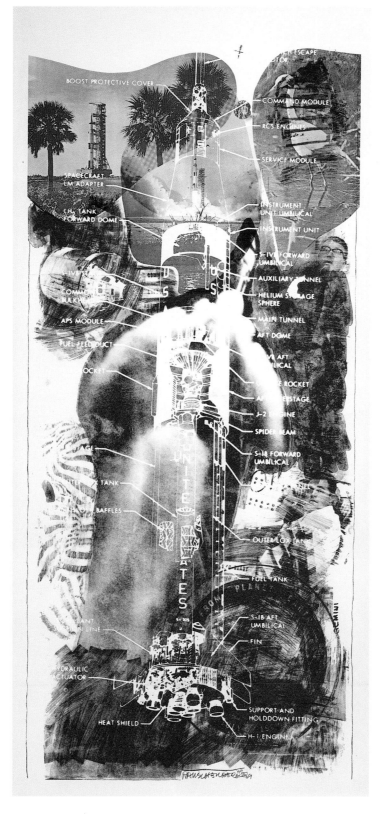

122. Robert Rauschenberg. *Sky Garden*. 1969. Published by
Gemini G.E.L. Lithograph and silkscreen, 84⅛ x 37⁵⁄₁₆″
(213.8 x 95.4 cm.) © copyright Gemini G.E.L., Los Angeles,
California, 1969

123. Robert Rauschenberg. *Page 2* from *Pages and Fuses*. 1974.
Published by Gemini G.E.L. Handmade paper, diam. 22" (55.9
cm.) © copyright Gemini G.E.L., Los Angeles, California, 1974

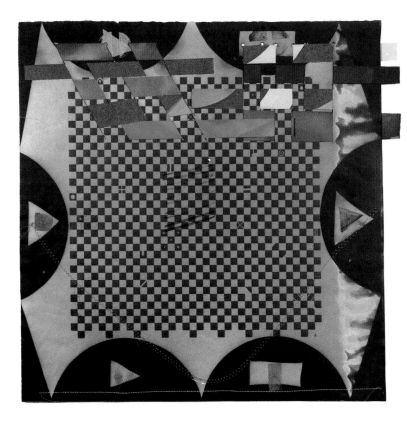

125. Frank Stella. *Lunna Wola*. 1975. Produced and
published by Tyler Graphics Ltd. Dyed and collaged
molded paper, hand-colored, 26 x 21½ x 1¾"
(66.0 x 54.6 x 4.4 cm.). © Frank Stella/Tyler
Graphics Ltd. 1975

124. Alan Shields. *Sun, Moon. Title Page*. 1971. Stencil on dyed,
cut, and sewn paper, 25¹⁵⁄₁₆ x 26⅛" (65.9 x 66 6 cm.). Paula
Cooper Gallery, New York

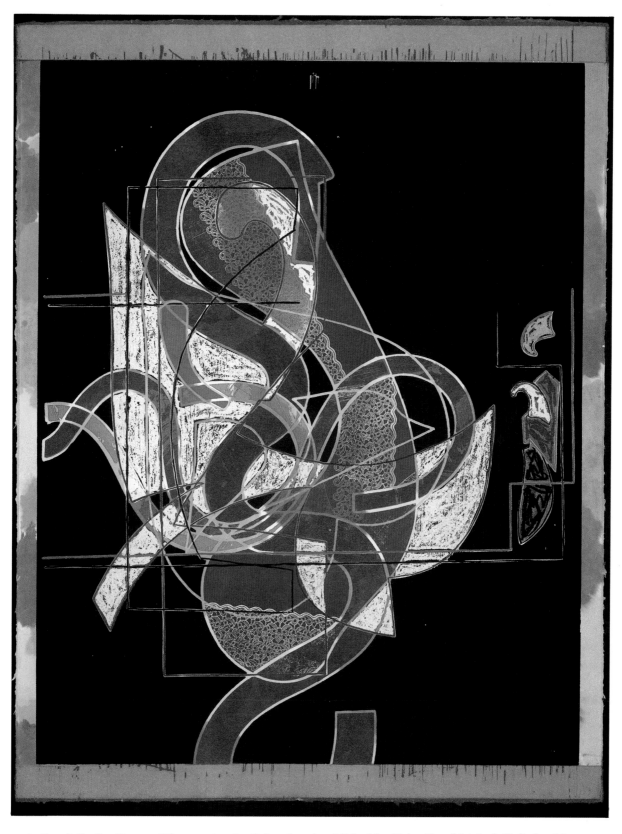

126. Frank Stella. *Pergusa Three*. 1982–83. Printed and published by Tyler Graphics Ltd. Relief etching and woodcut on colored paper, 66⅜ x 51½″ (168.6 x 130.8 cm.). © Frank Stella/Tyler Graphics Ltd. 1983

127. Sam Gilliam. *Nile*. 1972. Published by Impressions Workshop. Lithograph, printed on verso and folded, 24¹⁵⁄₁₆ x 17¹³⁄₁₆″ (63.3 x 45.3 cm.). Barbara Fendrick Gallery

128. Nancy Graves. *Muin*. 1977. Printed and published by Tyler Graphics Ltd. Etching, aquatint, and drypoint, 19¹⁵⁄₁₆ x 23¾″ (50.6 x 60.3 cm.). © Nancy Graves/Tyler Graphics Ltd. 1977

129. Richard Lindner. *Hit* from the portfolio *Fun City.*
1971. Published by Shorewood Publishers, Inc.
Lithograph and collotype on vinyl, 25⁵⁄₁₆ x 19¹³⁄₁₆″
(64.3 x 50.3 cm.). The Museum of Modern Art, New
York, gift of Richard Fleishmann

130. Romare Bearden. *The Train*, 1975.
Published by Transworld Art. Etching,
aquatint, and stencil, 17¹¹⁄₁₆ x 22⅛″
(44.9 x 56.2 cm.). The Museum of Modern
Art, New York

131. Saul Steinberg. *Sam's Art* from the portfolio *New York International*. (1966). Published by Tanglewood Press. Color lithograph, 15½ x 21¹⁵⁄₁₆″ (39.4 x 55.7 cm.). The Museum of Modern Art, New York, gift of Tanglewood Press

Generally thought of as a cartoonist, Saul Steinberg is known primarily for his archly laconic drawings on the covers of *The New Yorker* magazine. However, these works have been only part of an extensive creative production. His doodle-inspired creatures have been seen as both whimsical and socially critical, but in the main are the supreme examples of what the wandering mind can conjure. Steinberg's art not only has humor but also strong identification with the kind of scribbling that occupies bored minds and hands at business meetings and dull lectures: it is a style recognizably familiar to nearly everyone. The popularity of his work, especially during the 1960s, led several publishers to invite him to make prints. This lithograph is one of his first, printed by Irwin Hollander for Rosa Esman's second album. Although Steinberg used his facile pencil, crayon, and washes with great flair in the few prints he made, he never developed a rapport with either printer or workshop and returned to the medium only for specific projects. Steinberg presents an attitude toward his subjects appropriated by much younger artists in the late 1970s. His preoccupation with the stylized swirls and angles of fancy, if not mindless penmanship, has its equivalent in the work of the graffiti artists of the 1980s. The perpetrators of graffiti who transformed themselves into artists might not recognize Steinberg as their master, but the inspiration of boredom unites them.

132. William T. Wiley. *Seasonall Gate*. 1975. Copyright and published by Landfall Press, Inc., Chicago, Illinois. Etching, 24 x 18″ (61.0 x 45.7 cm.)

Once referred to as "Dude Ranch Dada," the work of California artist William T. Wiley traces the remnants of some American dreams in pleasantly disjointed hallucinations. Born in Indiana, Wiley brings a middle-American humor to his subjects, which range from a world of magic signs whose principal occupant is a sort of wizard (the artist) reminiscent of the wondrous Oz to the mystical territory of the "West" and its tales of Indians and cowboys. In 1972 Wiley began to make prints with Jack Lemon, a former Tamarind printer, at his Landfall Press in Chicago. One of his first lithographs, *Wizdumb*, was printed on chamois, evoking the symbolism of an Indian robe or tent cover. Like most of his work, the print shown here has an exaggerated, drawled, cryptic title incorporated into the composition, along with many other written comments, aphorisms, and even a rebus. The cowboy covers his mouth in a gesture of surprise or disbelief, as a horselike animal walks through a broken-down gate. In the traditionally designed alphabet of the cattle brand, the right-hand margin is marked "A Brand of Discrimination." Information that this print was begun in 1974 hints that the title might refer to the Watergate scandal. The total composition, appearing to be a page torn from a tattered notebook, is casual and utterly graphic. The cowboy can be only an American Everyman, narrating yet another episode in the human comedy.

133. Red Grooms. *Gertrude*. 1975. Published by Brooke Alexander, Inc. Lithograph, 18¾ x 19 x 9⅞″ (47.6 x 48.3 x 25.1 cm.)

134. David Hockney. *Joe with David Harte*. 1980. Printed and published by Tyler Graphics Ltd. Lithograph, 47 x 31⅝″ (119.4 x 81.0 cm.). © Copyright David Hockney/Tyler Graphics Ltd. 1980.

135. Roy Lichtenstein. *Dr. Waldmann*. 1980. Published by Gemini G.E.L. Woodcut, 35¹⁄₁₆ x 27½″ (89.1 x 69.8 cm.). © copyright Gemini G.E.L., Los Angeles, California, 1980

136. Jasper Johns. *Savarin Monotype*. 1982. Monotype over lithograph, sheet 50 x 38″ (127.0 x 96.5 cm.). Courtesy Universal Limited Art Editions, Inc.

137. Claes Oldenburg. *Double Screwarch Bridge,* State II. 1980. Published by Multiples Inc. Etching and aquatint, 24 x 51″ (61.0 x 129.5 cm.)

138. ABOVE Robert Kushner. *National Treasure*. 1981.
Lithograph, 67⅛ x 30⅛″ (170.1 x 76.2 cm.). Published
by Holly Solomon Editions Ltd. © Robert Kushner,
courtesy Holly Solomon Editions Ltd.

139. RIGHT Jim Dine. *Black and White Robe*. 1977.
Published by Pace Editions. Etching and lithograph,
41½ x 29⁵⁄₁₆″ (105.4 x 74.4 cm.)

140. Michael Mazur. *Wakeby Storm III (Morning Rain)*. 1983.
Monotype, 66 x 51" (167.7 x 129.5 cm.). Barbara Mathes Gallery,
New York

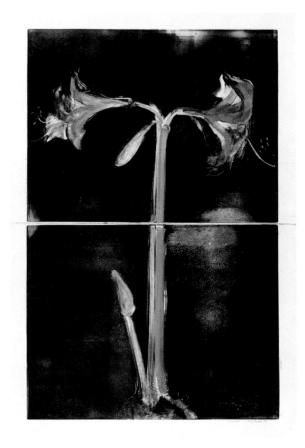

141. Mary Frank. *Amaryllis*. 1977. Monotype,
each plate 17¾ x 23¾" (45.1 x 60.3 cm.).
Metropolitan Museum of Art, New York,
Stewart S. MacDermott Fund

142. Philip Guston. *Coat.* 1980. Published by Gemini
G.E.L. Lithograph, 23¾ x 37⅝″ (60.3 x 95.6 cm.)
© copyright Gemini G.E.L., Los Angeles, California, 1980

143. Leon Golub. *Combat (I).* 1972. Photo-silkscreen,
44¹⁄₁₆ x 31″ (111.9 x 98.9 cm.). The Museum of Modern
Art, New York, John B. Turner Fund

144. Richard Bosman. *Drowning Man II*. 1981. Published by Brooke Alexander, Inc. Woodcut, 50⅟₁₆ x 24″ (101.8 x 61.0 cm.)

145. Susan Rothenberg. *Doubles*. 1980. Published by Multiples, Inc. Woodcut, 13¹⁄₁₆ x 30¹⁵⁄₁₆" (33.2 x 98.5 cm.)

146. Louisa Chase. *Chasm*. 1982. Published by Diane Villani. Woodcut, 23⅞ x 28"
(60.7 x 71.1 cm.)

147. Elizabeth Murray. Untitled. 1982. Co-published by the artist and Simca Print Artists, Inc. Silkscreen on three sheets, 48½ x 34¼″ (123.2 x 80.6 cm.)

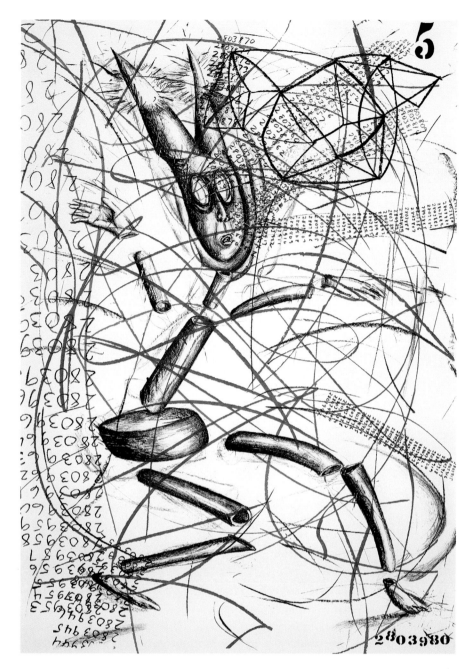

148. Jonathan Borofsky. *Stick Man*. 1983. Published by Gemini G.E.L. Lithograph, 52⁷⁄₁₆ x 37¹¹⁄₁₆″ (133.2 x 95.7 cm.). © copyright Gemini G.E.L., Los Angeles, California, 1983

The environmental works that added a special dimension to art in the 1970s and '80s, commandeering entire rooms instead of a few square feet, had many facets. In large spaces artists deployed sculptural structures, rigged tentlike enclosures, laid down tons of sanitized dirt, and set up other groupings of materials that, like a living room or office, could be experienced best by entering and moving around the objects. Jonathan Borofsky's environmental works are compiled from a diary-like recording of imagery and ideas that are given sequential numbers (as they have occurred to him). A slide made from one of his often dreamed-up images is projected on a wall or ceiling and traced there, while three-dimensional figures, enlarged and transformed in shape

through similar means, are incorporated into the total, somewhat topsy-turvy surroundings. One of the characters found in Borofsky's installations is depicted in this lithograph. Along the side of the print is a listing of the numbers that refer to Borofsky's notebook annotations and the various instances in which this strange amoeba-headed creature has been included. Typical of the art of the 1980s, Borofsky's prints are as diverse in style as the images he has borrowed or conjured. Rarely do the prints show more than one subject, which makes them more of an excerpt from a composition than a discrete work of art. It is clear from some of Borofsky's multiple works, however, that, like all his objects, they are meant to be added to others. The *Stick Man*, therefore, must be seen only as a participant in a larger scenario, which, if not provided by Borofsky, exists in the space in which it has been hung by its owner—or among these pages.

149. David Salle. Plate from *Until Photographs Could Be Taken from Earth Satellites*. 1981. Published by Parasol Press Ltd. Aquatint, 30 x 41″ (76.2 x 104.1 cm.). New York Public Library

150. Julian Schnabel. *Dream*. 1983. Published by Parasol Press Ltd. Sugar-lift etching, 54 x 72″ (137.2 x 182.9 cm.)

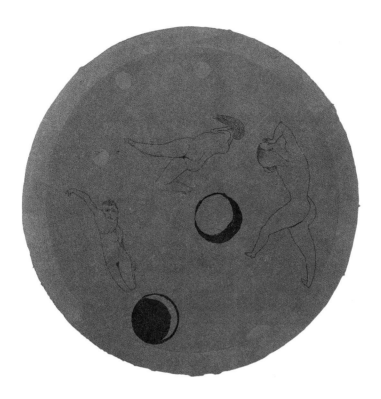

151. Francisco Clemente. *Tondo*. 1981. Published by Crown
Point Press. Etching and aquatint, diam. 16½″ (41.9 cm.)

AFTERWORD

In many ways the print workshop has come to control the how, when, and who of the process of creation. It seems unfortunate that there was no printer around in the 1940s and '50s to lead Rothko, Kline, or Gorky into the activity that has polished and extended the artistic careers of some of America's finest painters. The workshops have themselves become formidable resources for the continuation of many kinds of art activity. Even those artists who have equipped their own studios with printing paraphernalia and hired their own professional printers will go to an independent workshop for some projects.

The workshops are most often the initiators of these projects, inviting artists to undertake works that require new solutions, which then provide inspiration and impetus for still newer approaches. If, as in the past, most of today's printers had come from a craft-apprentice system, it is quite unlikely that most of the artists who have made prints in the past quarter-century would have done so. But the contemporary printer has first been trained as an artist, and has developed his skill in problem-solving in ways quite foreign to his predecessors. Most traditional printers maintained the ancient methods of etching and printing, but their modern American counterparts experiment in order to present artists with new techniques specifically geared to individual modes of expression.

The printer's role in production is usually acknowledged by an embossed seal (chop) in the margin of each print, while records are kept of the printing process, sometimes covering every detail, which are made available to the eventual owner. In this attention to documentation, very little information is given about the artist's involvement (whether a maquette or any other artwork served the artist or printer as a model for the print; in how many of the processes the artist participated) except that his or her signature in pencil on the paper seems to assure the work's originality. Unlike the prints of earlier centuries (which bore the names of artist, engraver, and printer), contemporary works are surrounded with a mass of data that reveals very little. All this mumbo jumbo has fogged our view of prints as objects of art, loading them with the burden of authenticity in order to protect the gullible—or as we now call it, consumer protection.

In the 1980s local laws were enacted in America that protect both artists and the public against misrepresentation of artworks. The unquantifiable barrage of information that ensues from confronting art with such laws forms yet another barrier to its appreciation. When so many of our most important artists have dedicated themselves to making prints, it is unpardonable that the insecurity that arises from the commercial aspects of the medium should obscure if not destroy its significance as art.

Notes, Bibliography, and Index

1. Alfred H. Barr, Jr., *What is Modern Painting?* (New York: Museum of Modern Art, 1943), p. 35. (Changed to "which in turn *tries* to defend itself" in the 1980 edition.)

2. Alvin Toffler, *Future Shock* (New York: Random House, 1970), p. 29.

3. J[ames] L[ane], review of Macmillan exhibition, *Art News*, January 15–31, 1942, p. 29.

4. Sylvan Cole, Jr., in "Symposium on American Prints, 1913–1963," Museum of Modern Art, New York, December 3, 1974 (unpublished transcript of the proceedings).

5. Sue Fuller, in ibid.

6. Kneeland McNulty, "A Decade of American Printmaking," *Philadelphia Museum Bulletin*, Autumn 1952, p. 15.

7. Robert Carleton Hobbs, "Early Abstract Expressionism: A Concern with the Unknown Within," in *Abstract Expressionism: The Formative Years*, exhibition catalogue, Herbert F. Johnson Museum of Art, Ithaca, New York, and Whitney Museum of American Art, New York, 1978, p. 20.

8. Ad Reinhardt, "Art as Art," *Art International*, December 1962, p. 20.

9. ". . . the 'message' of any medium or technology is the change of scale or pace or pattern that it introduces into human affairs." (Marshall McLuhan, *Understanding Media: The Extensions of Man*, 3rd paperback edition [New York: McGraw-Hill, 1966], p. 8.)

10. Cole, op. cit.

11. Ben Shahn, in *Ben Shahn*, exhibition catalogue, Downtown Gallery, New York, 1959.

BIBLIOGRAPHY

GENERAL

Clinton Adams. *American Lithographers, 1900–1960: Artists and Their Printers*. Albuquerque: University of New Mexico Press, 1983.

Gene Baro. *Graphicstudio U.S.F.: An Experiment in Art and Education*. Exhibition catalogue. Brooklyn: Brooklyn Museum, 1978.

Mary Welsh Baskett. *American Graphic Workshops: 1968*. Exhibition catalogue. Cincinnati: Cincinnati Art Museum, 1968.

Graham W. J. Beal. *Artist and Printer: Six American Print Studios*. Exhibition catalogue. Minneapolis: Walker Art Center, 1980.

E. Maurice Bloch. *Tamarind: A Renaissance of Lithography*. Exhibition catalogue. Washington, D.C.: International Exhibitions Foundation, 1971.

———. *Words and Images: Universal Limited Art Editions*. Exhibition catalogue. Los Angeles: University of Los Angeles Art Council, 1978.

Riva Castleman. *Technics and Creativity: Gemini G.E.L.* Exhibition catalogue. New York: Museum of Modern Art, 1971.

Richard Field. *Recent American Etching*. Exhibition catalogue. Washington, D.C.: National Collection of Fine Arts, Smithsonian Institution, 1975.

Peter Gale and Tony Towle. *Contemporary American Prints from Universal Limited Art Editions/The Rapp Collection*. Exhibition catalogue. Toronto: Art Gallery of Ontario, 1979.

Judith Goldman. *American Prints: Process and Proofs*. Exhibition catalogue. New York: Harper & Row, 1979.

———. *Art off the Picture Press: Tyler Graphics Ltd.* Exhibition catalogue. Hempstead, N.Y.: Emily Low Gallery, Hofstra University, 1977.

———. *Print Publishing in America*. Exhibition catalogue. Washington, D.C.: United States Communication Agency, 1980.

S. W. Hayter. *New Ways of Gravure*. New York: Pantheon, 1949.

Jules Heller. *Printmaking Today*. New York: Holt, Rinehart and Winston, 1972.

Una E. Johnson. *American Prints and Printmakers*. Garden City, N.Y.: Doubleday, 1980.

William S. Lieberman and Virginia Allen. *Tamarind: Homage to Lithography*. Exhibition catalogue. New York: Museum of Modern Art, 1969.

Lizbeth Marano. *Parasol and Simca: Two Presses/Two Processes*. Exhibition catalogue. Lewisburg, Pa.: Bucknell University Press, and Wilkes-Barre, Pa.: Wilkes College Press, 1984.

Joann Moser. *Atelier 17*. Exhibition catalogue. Madison: University of Wisconsin Press, Elvehjem Art Center, 1977.

Nancy Tousley. *Prints: Bochner, LeWitt, Mangold, Marden, Martin, Renouf, Rockburne, Ryman*. Exhibition catalogue. Toronto: Art Gallery of Ontario, 1975.

James Watrous. *A Century of American Printmaking, 1880–1980*. Madison: University of Wisconsin Press, 1984.

MONOGRAPHS

Jo Miller. *Josef Albers: Prints, 1915–1976*. Brooklyn: Brooklyn Museum, 1973.

Arakawa: Print Works, 1965–1979. Kitakyushu, Japan: Kitakyushu City Museum of Art, 1979.

Una E. Johnson and Jo Miller. *Milton Avery: Prints and Drawings, 1930–1964*. Brooklyn: Brooklyn Museum, 1966.

Leonard Baskin: The Graphic Work, 1950–70. New York: FAR Gallery, 1970.

Kurt Gallwitz. *Max Beckmann: Die Druckgraphik, 1910–1948*. Karlsruhe: Badischer Kunstverein, 1962.

Richard S. Field. *Prints and Drawings by Lee Bontecou*. Middletown, Conn.: Wesleyan University Press, 1975.

Elke Solomon. *Chryssa: Selected Prints and Drawings,*

1959–1962. New York: Whitney Museum of American Art, 1972.

Richard B. Freeman. *The Lithographs of Ralston Crawford*. Louisville: University of Kentucky Press, 1962.

Mark Stevens. *Richard Diebenkorn: Etchings and Drypoints, 1949–1980*. Houston: Houston Fine Arts Press, 1981.

Jim Dine: Complete Graphics. Berlin: Galerie Mikro, 1970.

Thomas Krens. *Jim Dine's Prints*. New York: Harper & Row, in association with the Williams College Artist-in-Residence Program, 1977.

———. *Helen Frankenthaler: Prints, 1961–1979*. New York: Harper & Row, 1979.

Nat Hentoff and Charles Parkhurst. *Frasconi Against the Grain: The Woodcuts of Antonio Frasconi*. New York: Macmillan, 1972.

Michael Mazur. "The Monoprints of Naum Gabo," *Print Collectors Newsletter* 9:5 (November–December 1978): 148–51.

Paul Richard. *Red Grooms: A Catalogue Raisonné of His Graphic Work, 1957–1981*. Nashville, Tenn.: Fine Arts Center, 1981.

Charles Goerg. *Stanley William Hayter: 40 ans de gravure*. Geneva: Cabinet des Estampes, Musée d'Art et d'Histoire, 1966.

William Katz. *Robert Indiana: The Prints and Posters, 1961–1971*. Stuttgart and New York: Edition Domberger, 1971.

Richard S. Field. *Jasper Johns: Prints, 1960–1970*. Philadelphia: Museum of Art, 1970.

———. *Jasper Johns: Prints, 1970–1977*. Middletown, Conn.: Wesleyan University Press, 1978.

Elke Solomon and Richard S. Field. *Alex Katz: Prints*. New York: Whitney Museum of American Art, 1974.

Diane Waldman. *Ellsworth Kelly: Drawings, Collages, Prints*. Greenwich, Conn.: New York Graphic Society, 1971.

R. B. Kitaj: Complete Graphics, 1964–69. Berlin: Galerie Mikro, 1969.

Joann Moser, Michael Danoff, and Jan K. Muhlert. *Mauricio Lasansky*. Iowa City: University of Iowa Press, 1976.

Sol LeWitt: Graphik, 1970–1975. Basel: Kunsthalle, and Bern: Verlag Kornfeld, 1975.

Diane Waldman. *Roy Lichtenstein: Drawings and Prints*. New York: Chelsea House, 1972.

John Loring. *Marisol: Prints, 1961–1973*. New York: New York Cultural Center, 1973.

Stephanie Terenzio. *The Painter and the Printer: Robert Motherwell's Graphics, 1943–1980*, with catalogue raisonné by Dorothy C. Belknap. New York: American Federation of Arts, 1980.

Gene Baro. *Nevelson: The Prints*. New York: Pace Editions, 1974.

Hugh Davies and Riva Castleman. *The Prints of Barnett Newman*. New York: Barnett Newman Foundation, 1983.

Gene Baro. *Claes Oldenburg: Drawings and Prints*. New York: Chelsea House, 1969.

Claes Oldenburg: Drawings, Watercolors, and Prints. Stockholm: Moderna Museet, 1977.

Richard S. Field. *The Lithographs and Etchings of Philip Pearlstein*. Springfield, Mo.: Springfield Art Museum, 1978.

Una E. Johnson. *Gabor Peterdi: Graphics, 1934–1969*. New York: Touchstone Publishers, 1970.

Francis V. O'Connor and Eugene V. Thaw. *Jackson Pollock: A Catalogue Raisonné of Prints, Drawings and Other Works*. New Haven: Yale University Press, 1978.

E. A. Foster. *Robert Rauschenberg: Prints, 1948–1970*. Minneapolis: Institute of Art, 1970.

James Rosenquist: Graphics Retrospective. Sarasota, Fla.: John and Mable Ringling Museum of Art, 1979.

Graphic Works by Edward Ruscha. Auckland: Auckland City Art Museum, 1978.

Una E. Johnson and Jo Miller. *Louis Schanker: Prints, 1924–1971*. Brooklyn: Brooklyn Museum, 1974.

Rainer Michael Mason. *Kurt Seligmann: Oeuvre gravé*. Geneva: Editions du Tricorne, 1982.

Kenneth Prescott. *The Complete Graphic Works of Ben Shahn*. New York: Quadrangle, 1973.

Richard Axsom. *The Prints of Frank Stella: A Catalogue Raisonné, 1967–1982*. New York: Hudson Hills Press, 1983.

Gene Baro. *Carol Summers: Woodcuts*. San Francisco: A.D.I. Gallery, 1977

Wolfgang Wittrock. *Yves Tanguy: Das Druckgraphische Werk*. Düsseldorf: Wittrock, 1976.

Wayne Thiebaud: Graphics, 1967–1971. New York: Parasol Press, 1971.

Kristen Spangenberg. *Mark Tobey: A Decade of Printmaking*. Cincinnati: Cincinnati Art Museum, 1972.

Hermann Wünsche. *Andy Warhol: Das Graphische Werk, 1962–1980*. Bonn: n.p., n.d.

Mary W. Baskett. *The Art of June Wayne*. New York: Harry N. Abrams, 1969.

Tom Wesselmann: Graphics, 1964–1977. Boston: Institute of Contemporary Art, 1978.

A NOTE ABOUT THE AUTHOR

Riva Castleman is Director of the Department of Prints and Illustrated Books at The Museum of Modern Art in New York City. She has been a member of the department's staff since 1963 and has supervised it since 1971, being named Director in 1976. During her tenure she has organized exhibitions of prints by Josef Albers, Pierre Alechinsky, Arakawa, Jim Dine, Jasper Johns, Henri Matisse, Joan Miro, Edvard Munch, and Pablo Picasso. She has also directed several comprehensive surveys of modern prints that have traveled to cities in Europe, Asia, Australia, and New Zealand. She participates in the selection of American representation in several major international print biennials and serves on the juries of others.

Riva Castleman's previous publications include *Technics and Creativity: Gemini G.E.L.*; *Modern Art in Prints*; *Contemporary Prints*; *Prints of the 20th Century: A History*; *Printed Art: A View of Two Decades*; *Modern Artists as Illustrators*; and *Prints from Blocks: Gauguin to Now*.

A NOTE ON THE TYPE

The text of this book was set in Bembo, a facsimile of a typeface cut by
one of the most celebrated goldsmiths of his time, Francesco Griffo, for
Aldus Manutius, the Venetian printer, in 1495. The face was named for
Pietro Bembo, the author of the small treatise entitled *De Ætna*, in
which it first appeared. Through the research of Stanley Morison, it is
now acknowledged that all old-face type designs up to the time of
William Caslon can be traced to the Bembo cut.

The present-day version of Bembo was introduced by The Monotype Corporation, London, in 1929. Sturdy, well balanced, and finely
proportioned, Bembo is a face of rare beauty and great legibility in all
of its sizes.

Composition by Graphic Composition, Inc., Athens, Georgia
Separations, printing and binding by Toppan Printing Co., Inc.,
    Tokyo, Japan
Designed by Holly McNeely